NEW DIMENSIONS OF
CHINA-JAPAN-U.S. RELATIONS

The Japan Center for International Exchange wishes to thank

Henry Luce Foundation, Inc.

United States Institute of Peace

NEW DIMENSIONS OF CHINA-JAPAN-U.S. RELATIONS

edited by
Japan Center for International Exchange

JCIE

Tokyo • Japan Center for International Exchange • *New York*

The surnames of the authors and other persons mentioned in this book are positioned according to country practice.

Copyediting by Pamela J. Noda.
Cover and typographic design by Becky Davis, EDS Inc., Editorial & Design Services, Tokyo. Typesetting and production by EDS Inc.

Printed in Japan
ISBN 4-88907-028-1

Distributed worldwide outside Japan by Brookings Institution Press, 1775 Massachusetts Avenue, N.W., Washington, D.C. 20036-2188 U.S.A.

Japan Center for International Exchange
9-17 Minami Azabu 4-chome, Minato-ku, Tokyo 106-0047 Japan
URL: http://www.jcie.or.jp

Japan Center for International Exchange, Inc. (JCIE/USA)
1251 Avenue of the Americas, New York, N.Y. 10020 U.S.A.

Contents

Foreword

TODAY IT IS WIDELY RECOGNIZED that the continuing security and prosperity of the Asia Pacific region, acknowledged as the most dynamic region of the world in the twenty-first century despite its recent setback, will be largely contingent upon enhanced cooperation among the region's three dominant economies: China, Japan, and the United States. The China-Japan-U.S. Research and Dialogue Project to study the trilateral relationship was conceived by several individuals representing policy research institutions in the three countries who believed that promoting joint analysis and dialogue among them would be critical and essential in managing the future trilateral relationship. The project consists of a parent group of senior leading policy thinkers from the three countries and three study groups of emerging intellectual leaders from each country. The parent group launched the project with a workshop in Beijing in December 1996. This was followed by creation of the study group of young Japanese scholars and researchers who participated in monthly study meetings in Japan and also took part in a dialogue mission to Beijing, Hong Kong, and Shanghai in December 1996. The study group of emerging Chinese leaders was also established and they participated in a dialogue mission to Tokyo in June 1997. The volume of essays by the three international relations experts in the parent group, titled *China-Japan-U.S.: Managing the Trilateral Relationship*, was published in 1998; the collection of essays by the group of younger Japanese intellectual leaders, titled *Challenges for China-Japan-U.S. Cooperation*, was also published that year (both books are distributed worldwide outside Japan by the Brookings Institution Press).

The activities of the group of young American researchers and scholars began with a conference in Washington, D.C., on July 9–11, 1998. Senior members of the China-Japan-U.S. Research and Dialogue Project also attended the Washington conference. The conference was sponsored by the Japan Center for International Exchange (JCIE) on the Japan side in collaboration with the Institute of American Studies of the Chinese Academy of Social Sciences and the Chinese Reform Forum on the Chinese side and the United States Institute of Peace on the U.S. side. Discussion centered on such issues as developments in the China-Japan-U.S. relationship observed since the group last met in Tokyo in June 1997; implications of the Asian financial crisis, which has affected the relationship between the three countries; and the impact on trilateral relations of other international events such as the nuclear tests in India and Pakistan and developments on the Korean peninsula. This volume is a collection of essays first presented at the conference and later revised and updated for publication.

The China-Japan-U.S. Research and Dialogue Project is a key activity under the Global ThinkNet scheme launched by JCIE in 1996. The Global ThinkNet—made possible by the generous support of the Nippon Foundation—is a multipronged cluster of policy research and dialogue activities designed to contribute to strengthening the Asia Pacific as well as the global intellectual policy network among research institutions and intellectual leaders.

JCIE wishes to express its sincere gratitude to the Nippon Foundation and the Henry Luce Foundation, Inc., for their financial support for the Washington conference. JCIE is also grateful to the United States Institute of Peace and the Asia Pacific Agenda Project for their contribution.

YAMAMOTO TADASHI
President
Japan Center for International Exchange

NEW DIMENSIONS OF
CHINA-JAPAN-U.S. RELATIONS

CHAPTER I

Introduction: Prospects for a China-Japan-U.S. Trilateral Dialogue

Scott Snyder

THE EXCHANGE OF SUMMITS between China and the United States, the Asian financial crisis, and the decisions by India and Pakistan to engage in nuclear testing redirected the security agenda of the Asia Pacific region in 1998. These developments underscored the difficulties inherent in the transition from the traditional approaches to security as defined by the cold war to a post–cold war structure of international relations in the Asia Pacific region. To varying degrees, China, Japan, and the United States are all being forced to address a new agenda based on the emerging priorities of the post–cold war era. However, each of these countries is unwilling to abandon the familiar and comfortable old structure, including the historical grievances, dependencies, and nationalist rivalries that defined relations in the past.

The major challenge is management of the positive transition to a stable and cooperative set of regional relationships while not inflaming the tensions of the past. One vehicle for addressing the problems of the future while simultaneously confronting past legacies would be a three-way dialogue among China, Japan, and the United States—the three countries with the greatest influence in the Asia Pacific region.

A sense of rapid change resulting from the Asian financial crisis and other unexpected events has resulted in a difficult environment in which to develop long-term strategy. However, the failure to articulate a strategy increases ambivalence among specialists and policymakers in China, Japan, and the United States, creating greater potential for misperceptions that might lead to miscalculation or misunderstanding.

For example, Chinese leaders recognize the importance of improving relations with the United States with an eye to avoiding the policy failures of Indonesia's political leadership while also looking over their shoulders at a Japan adrift: Beijing contends that leadership in Tokyo is desperately needed but worries that real leadership in Japan could lead to greater political and security independence that might challenge China's own future aspirations to regional leadership. Japan's economic muddle draws its political leaders inward just as its neighbors are calling for decisive leadership to pull Asia's economies out of stagnation. U.S. analysts weigh images of a China rising against the current formidable difficulties of economic reform with that country's limited space for political expression. To the extent that the respective political leaderships can shape policies rather than allowing their choices to be dictated by external circumstances, uncertainty regarding intentions and aspirations may be decreased.

CHALLENGES OF POST–COLD WAR LEADERSHIP

The state faces unprecedented challenges to its ability to provide leadership in the modern era. A widening array of nonstate actors have gained influence that can be used either to support or to challenge the central government's leadership. The understanding and careful cultivation of these new constituencies have become prerequisites for successful leadership, even in countries with relatively controlled political environments. As coercion is neither a viable nor a desirable option, state leaders must master the art of persuasion in both domestic and international affairs, wooing "coalitions of the willing" both to gain domestic support and to broaden support at the international level.

The exponential increase in the global flow of information and

capital has given increased prominence to new international constituencies—for example, the market and the media—as groups that
must be cultivated to sustain political power. And the influence of
perceptions may overwhelm substance as pressure increases to make
significant policy decisions quickly and usually without all of the facts
in hand. Ironically, these newly emerging constituencies must be both
courted and resisted as part of a strategy for effective leadership. Con-
sistency and vision are particularly prized because they appear to be
in such short supply. Interestingly, newly emerging shared challenges
to political leadership may provide a pretext for enhanced policy coordination among state leaders in China, Japan, and the United
States.

The remarkable reversal of capital flows that occurred in conjunc-
tion with the Asian financial crisis constituted a major shock to the
Asian economic infrastructure, unveiling secretive backroom business deals and putting a premium on transparency and the timely
provision of accurate information as the new requirements necessary to build and maintain the confidence of global financial markets. Policymakers in Beijing must recognize that opening markets
and eliminating corruption are necessary and inevitable; the issue is
how to manage such a process orderly and efficiently. To the extent
that policymakers in Tokyo or elsewhere have been unwilling to come
clean regarding the extent of the crisis, it has only delayed prospects
for economic recovery. And, despite some conspiracy theories tar-
geting the U.S. Treasury as the evil manipulator of the global economic order, U.S. policymakers find themselves captive to market
forces and are well aware of the dangers of recklessly exposing the
limitations of their own leadership in cases where the market may be
unwilling to follow.

Nonstate actors and nongovernmental organizations have reached
across international borders to press their concerns more effectively.
The global effort to ban land mines may be the most effective international example, but regionally the campaign for recognition
and compensation from the Japanese government led by "comfort
women" in China, South Korea, and Southeast Asia has influenced
government policy formation in Asia. At the same time, the institutionalization of the World Trade Organization (WTO), even as
China continues to negotiate the terms of its own membership, has

limited the freedom of unilateral policy action by governments, including the United States, replacing bilateralism with an international court for the equitable settlement of trade disputes. Although governments may attempt to limit citizen contacts across borders by regulating information flows through the Internet, globalization is "the wave of the future," and no country can resist it without paying the inordinate costs of isolation.

Domestic political constraints have limited effective cooperation at the international level. Political leaders in China, Japan, and the United States have found their freedom of action on the international stage constrained by domestic politics, such as the continuing popular Chinese resentment toward the history of Japanese aggression during World War II, the perplexities of perpetuating local pork projects contrary to necessary financial reforms in Japan, or the ugly politics surrounding sex scandals in Washington.

Ironically, the common challenges to governance may bring national leaders closer as they consider how to broaden the foundations of leadership despite these new challenges. Joint intervention by the Federal Reserve Bank and Japan's Ministry of Finance in June 1998 was stimulated partially by concerns that further devaluation of the yen might also cause China to devalue its currency, unleashing a new round of "beggar-thy-neighbor" currency devaluations that might trigger global deflation. Although China's decision not to devalue the renminbi may have been in its own economic interests, the Chinese leadership gained significant political benefits from stepped-up consultations with its neighbors and its reassurances that it would stand firm despite reduced foreign investment flows to the Chinese mainland. The United States has led a new round of financial consultations among the G-22 in Asia, simultaneously consulting on pressing issues resulting from the crisis and discussing adjustments in the global financial architecture that might stem the recurrence of such a crisis.

ENHANCED TRILATERAL COOPERATION OUT OF THE ASIAN FINANCIAL CRISIS?

The dilemmas posed by the Asian financial crisis have required enhanced coordination efforts involving the U.S. Treasury in dialogue with its counterparts in China and Japan. Although many of these efforts have involved joint coordination and technical support to manage short-term macroeconomic responses to the challenges posed by the crisis, the United States has engaged in overt and indirect forms of *gaiatsu* to mobilize a response to structural problems of immediate concern, particularly in the case of Japan. Indeed, the crisis has revived the Asian values debate, with critics quick to point out shortcomings in the Japanese economic model.

Although the fundamental task in responding to the Asian financial crisis remains that of restoring confidence through transparency, strong prudential regulation, and the willingness to admit and allow the failure and restructuring of bankrupt institutions, the critical issues posed by the crisis may differ depending on the stage of economic development. For instance, China's long-term difficulties focus on the challenge of making its currency convertible while concurrently reforming inefficient state-owned enterprises; the Asian financial crisis has narrowed the margin of error for successfully managing this task while signaling useful lessons for China to avoid from the Japanese and South Korean experiences. Crisis impels progress in instigating reforms necessary to move to the next stage of development, at which point a country might face different types of crisis and new imperatives for reform, as the Japanese situation suggests.

Although coordination has been the theme of consultations between economic officials in China and the United States, *gaiatsu* has been the byword that describes the much more intertwined and deeper level of consultation between the U.S. Treasury and the Ministry of Finance. External pressure from the United States is partially a result of America's profound interest in having Japan deal with its problems so as to halt the contagion effect on the global economy, including the United States. Thus, pressure in the current crisis is more a feature of the closeness of Japan-U.S. relations than a symbol of fraying or distance. Also, U.S. pressure has become a familiar and expected part of the Japanese policy-making process. Domestic constituencies in Japan that favor reform need external support to overcome the entrenched self-interests of a bureaucratic structure that, although highly successful in the past, has failed to choose correct macroeconomic policies in the 1990s.

Does Japan's current stagnation presage the failure of the Asian economic model for growth? And are Japan's current economic difficulties insurmountable? Observers are encouraged to look beyond the vagaries of the business cycle. During the 1980s, the United States was in the economic doldrums as a result of its savings-and-loan crisis, whereas Japan and others provided a small measure of reverse *gaiatsu* through criticism of the ballooning U.S. budget deficits. Japan's economic performance in the 1990s may be similar in many respects, but Japan should not be counted out in the future.

Likewise, the debate over the role of government planning or public subsidies as a means by which to target or enhance economic performance and efficiency will not likely be settled soon. In some cases, public regulations fetter the efficiencies of the market; however, government must provide regulatory oversight in such a way as to enhance those efficiencies and augment national competitiveness. The debate over how to reform the regulatory architecture for managing global capital flows reflects the same debate over the extent that regulatory mechanisms are necessary or desirable. Would intervention to determine a fixed yen/dollar exchange rate, for instance, resolve the current crisis of confidence, or would the inefficiencies that might result actually limit the potential for additional capital formation needed to escape the crisis? In reality, the Asian and U.S. models are mixed, as are the various contrasting organizational cultures even within the same industrial sectors in the United States; for example, the East Coast high-tech organizational culture is different and less efficient than that of Silicon Valley, which, at first glance, seems to share more Asian characteristics.

To address the long-term economic and financial problems more effectively, coordination mechanisms should be established that include all the right players. China's admission to the WTO might be one step in that direction, if leaders in Beijing can effect the necessary internal economic reforms to meet qualifications for WTO membership. Given China's emerging importance and its responsible, if self-interested, economic behavior in response to the Asian financial crisis, would China's inclusion in the G-8 make that organization more effective? Is the current level of consultation among Asian financial and banking officials sufficient? In addition to China-U.S. consultations over economic matters, should Sino-Japanese economic consultations be stepped up on a wider variety of issues, or would a trilateral economic discussion of regional trends be of value?

TRILATERAL COOPERATION AND REGIONAL SECURITY ISSUES

In principle, it is in the interest of China, Japan, and the United States to cooperate in efforts to resolve and prevent regional conflicts, for example, on the Korean peninsula and in South Asia, as well as to ensure that cross-strait differences between Beijing and Taipei do not escalate tensions that might draw in external actors such as the United States to keep the peace. In practice, however, uncertainties about the future may limit practical cooperation measures in areas where long-term national interests may conflict. Indeed, major power cooperation might hinder progress if directly concerned parties feel that their own interests are being ignored.

China, Japan, and the United States have a near-term interest in maintaining stability on the Korean peninsula. In fact, neither of the two Koreas seems eager for sudden or destabilizing events that might lead to German-style reunification in the aftermath of the Asian financial crisis and the election of South Korean President Kim Dae Jung. However, major power cooperation in managing policies toward the Korean peninsula currently takes the form of complementary and reinforcing parallel actions rather than direct or institutionalized coordination.

For instance, the Korean Peninsula Energy Development Organization (KEDO) is an international organization formed to provide light-water reactors to North Korea in return for the dismantling of North Korea's nuclear weapons program. Japan, the United States, and South Korea are core members, and the European Union has also joined. China, which also supports a nonnuclear Korean peninsula, claims that its contributions are most effective outside of KEDO. China's major food relief contributions are widely perceived as essential to perpetuating North Korea's survival, but they have been provided independent of international efforts through the UN World

Food Program. Japan, on the other hand, has been a remarkably passive actor—excepting its participation in KEDO—providing virtually no food assistance to North Korea despite its large rice stockpiles. In addition, Japan is excluded from the Four-Party Talks, even though Japan might be expected to provide financing to support a Korean peace process.

The challenge to the global nonproliferation regime posed by nuclear testing in India and Pakistan has also created opportunities for international consultation among China, Japan, and the United States. The "danger and opportunity" inherent in the South Asian nuclear crisis has, however, been poorly exploited, demonstrating the difficulties and potential for missteps that can accompany dialogue from which interested or reluctant parties are excluded.

Some observers have questioned whether the China-U.S. joint statement condemning South Asia's nuclear tests might have been premature in the absence of a broadly supported international formula accepted by India and Pakistan that effectively addresses proliferation issues. Without such a formula, a constructive process for managing the effects of proliferation in South Asia seems unlikely. Likewise, China's decision to exclude Japan from the UN-sponsored effort to draw the UN Security Council nuclear "haves" into a dialogue on nonproliferation that would also include India, Pakistan, and Israel constitutes a failure to enhance trilateral dialogue opportunities. Excluding Japan, which has shown responsibility by foregoing nuclear weapons development efforts, from international proliferation dialogue efforts is shortsighted because it punishes Japan for voluntary adherence to the values of the nonproliferation regime and reinforces the notion that nuclear weapons development is indeed a prerequisite for gaining leadership in international conclaves. A coordinated trilateral approach by China, Japan, and the United States that seeks to engage South Asian nuclear powers in confidence-building regimes and otherwise seeks to dampen South Asia's regional tensions might contribute constructively to international nonproliferation efforts.

Finally, cross-strait relations remain a sensitive issue in Beijing with ramifications for trilateral dialogue; indeed, Taiwan's leaders must also be constructively engaged for such consultations to bear fruit. To the extent that cross-strait relations improve, one might expect the Taiwan question to become less important as a subject of dialogue among Beijing, Tokyo, and Washington. However, it continues to be one of the most sensitive issues in China-U.S. and Sino-Japanese relations because it has been politicized and has taken on significance in political debates in all three capitals. The competition for support in international forums between Beijing and Taipei internationalizes the issue, yet Beijing continuously warns against "outside interference" on cross-strait relations.

Trilateral dialogue on this sensitive issue is valuable precisely because Taiwan represents the unresolved historical legacy of great power conflicts in Asia in the twentieth century, originating from the Sino-Japanese War of 1894–1895 in which Taiwan became a protectorate of Japan. And Taiwan's return to China was in the view of many in Beijing thwarted by U.S. cold war intervention and the heating up of the Korean War, as a result of which Mao Zedong failed to gain absolute and unconditional victory over the Chinese nationalists, leaving China divided. Resolution of such deep differences will take time and can only occur through careful consultations.

SINO-JAPANESE DIALOGUE

As the weakest bilateral link in the triangular relationship, Sino-Japanese cooperation may require special efforts to improve and broaden the agenda. It is particularly important that the recent warming of relations between Beijing and Washington also be reflected in Sino-Japanese relations; otherwise, China might become a controversial issue in Japan-U.S. relations. In fact, President Bill Clinton's sustained attention to China has become an issue requiring reassurance and explanation by U.S. officials visiting Tokyo.

The central task for Chinese and Japanese policymakers will be to define expectations for the future of Sino-Japanese relations in the context of other Chinese relationships. The agenda for such a relationship must be defined more broadly and more strategically than simply returning to the issues of Japan's historical legacy and Taiwan. It also requires the active development and articulation of a clear Japanese diplomatic strategy for overcoming historical legacies and managing more normal relationships in the region. How Beijing and

Tokyo might develop a common agenda that contributes to the perpetuation of peace, prosperity, and stability in the Asia Pacific region could be a key factor in determining the shape of regional relations in the twenty-first century.

CONCLUSION: PSYCHOLOGY OF TRILATERAL RELATIONS

The Asian financial crisis, the South Asian nuclear tests, and President Clinton's June 1998 visit to China appear to have drastically changed the context for discussion of trilateral relations, but these events underscored the fundamental premises behind the need for a three-way dialogue. In particular, concerns regarding the collateral effects of efforts to "demonize" China in Japan and the United States that were of concern in previous trilateral discussions have given way to questions about whether the United States might make a strategic choice to downplay or abandon its close security and economic relations with Japan in favor of a broadened and deepened relationship with a rising China in the next century. The facts suggest that to view U.S. options in these terms is both a false choice and, at best, a premature and unwise consideration under current circumstances. A deeply intertwined Japan-U.S. security relationship is based on decades of economic, security, and political investments, and shared democratic values. Japan-U.S. economic ties dwarf the China-U.S. economic relationship, even if China has caught up with Japan in terms of a bilateral trade surplus with the United States.

Perhaps more significant, manifestations of China's rise, particularly if it is perceived as having come about at Japan's expense, will raise questions regarding whether the ultimate objective of a trilateral dialogue is to develop equidistant tripartite relations or to reinforce current bilateral relationships while maintaining the status quo, in which the Japan-U.S. security relationship would always be shorter than the China-U.S. side of the triangle. Although such long-term direction will likely be influenced by domestic political activity or by the emergence of new regional challenges, trilateral dialogue is an appropriate outlet through which to increase confidence-building measures and enhance transparency among all of the parties precisely to forestall the suspicions that might develop if only bilateral contacts are fostered. In the case of either the perpetuation of the status quo through continued preeminence of Japan-U.S. security relations or the possible long-term development of an equidistant tripartite relationship in which Japan would become a more independent actor, the development of a sustained trilateral dialogue will be necessary to manage the psychology of trilateral relations so that one party does not feel that developments in bilateral relations are coming at the expense of any third party. The provision of such reassurance is the foremost task of such tripartite cooperation. Clearly, a need exists to further develop a constructive trilateral dialogue among China, Japan, and the United States.

CHAPTER II

Progress, Problems, and Trends

Yang Jiemian

RELATIONS AMONG China, Japan, and the United States are critical to global and regional developments. On the one hand, the trilateral relationship is undergoing some encouraging and positive readjustments, while on the other hand the three countries still have fundamental differences. Indeed, progress and problems tend to coexist in trilateral relations.

With the current trend favoring peace and development, the international environment as a whole is conducive to cooperation among these three major countries. The world is moving toward multipolarity but at a slower pace than before the Asian financial crisis. The financial crisis, which started in Thailand in July 1997, quickly spread to other Asian countries, thus bringing to a halt decades of rapid economic growth in the Asia Pacific region. China, Japan, and the United States—all major global powers—have bilateral and/or trilateral relations that are closely linked to development around the world. However, their major focus of interaction is in the Asia Pacific region.

During the transition to a multipolar world order, China, Japan, and the United States are governed by a combination of old and new ideas and beliefs. Some ideologues hold that the Japan-U.S. relationship is between two democracies, whereas the China-U.S. relationship is between a totalitarian country and a democratic country.

Geostrategists, on the other hand, posit that China-U.S. relations are likely to surpass Japan-U.S. relations in significance in the near future. These views have somewhat confused the public and have influenced government policies suitable for the new realities. However, in general the recent trend in trilateral relations emphasizes consultation, coordination, and cooperation.

In the past year, the United States continued to enjoy steady economic growth and to display a commanding lead in such areas as the telecommunications and information industries. Some analysts, nonplused by the staying power of this "new economy," are even questioning if the U.S. economy will again experience typical business cycles. The Clinton administration has also achieved some progress in foreign policy—in Bosnia and with North Atlantic Treaty Organization (NATO) expansion. Nevertheless, although the United States remains the world's sole superpower its ability to control world affairs is declining.

China continues to pursue reform and more open policies. Its continued rise as a global power has become irrefutable. In the past year, China not only has improved its relations with both Japan and the United States but also has nurtured its relationships with other small and medium-sized countries in the Asia Pacific region. China's prudent handling of the Hong Kong reversion and resolute shouldering of responsibility in the ongoing Asian financial crisis have won it general admiration in the international community.

Japan, however, continues to be beset by a weak and divided leadership and a troubled economy. It has been criticized as being irresponsible in international affairs for its conduct vis-à-vis the Asia financial crisis. In terms of the trilateral relationship, Japan has keenly observed, and with some apprehension, the recent rapprochement between China and the United States. Following President Bill Clinton's decision not to stop in Japan during his China trip and the China-U.S. initiative that excluded Japan from multilateral discussions of the South Asian nuclear crisis, Japan appears to be rudderless in its international affairs, expressing its obvious displeasure with recent events by criticizing what it refers to as "Japan passing."

Given these circumstances, the bilateral and trilateral relations of China, Japan, and the United States are in transition. Although the Japan-U.S. relationship still serves as the cornerstone of the United

States' Asia Pacific policy, the improvement in China-U.S. relations, as symbolized by the exchange of state visits by Presidents Jiang Zemin and Clinton, has narrowed the gap with the Japan-U.S. link. Sino-Japanese relations, despite occasional setbacks and difficulties, are generally improving. Indeed, the three countries are exploring ways to further improve their trilateral relations.

Of course, there are other players to consider in Asia Pacific affairs. Russia has recently refrained from playing a major role because of its domestic troubles. The Association of Southeast Asian Nations (ASEAN) has kept a somewhat low profile as its member countries are concentrating on internal affairs in the wake of the Asian financial crisis. Recent nuclear tests have made South Asia more prominent in global and regional affairs, and the Korean peninsula remains a trouble spot. The influence of these countries complicates the China-Japan-U.S. relationship. However, on balance these nations play more of a positive than a negative role in promoting improved cooperation among China, Japan, and the United States.

Some recent events, particularly the Asian financial crisis, the Iraqi chemical weapons inspection fracas, and the South Asian nuclear tests, have required China, Japan, and the United States to extend mutual consultation and cooperation. Significantly, the three countries for the first time not only are able to but also must coordinate their economic and financial policies. This may usher in a new era in which the three will establish a necessary framework for consultation and coordination in a variety of fields.

China's Enhanced Role

China's domestic situation and elevated international status have further improved its position vis-à-vis Japan and the United States. Recently, China smoothly regained sovereignty over Hong Kong in adherence to its principle of "one country, two systems," and the Chinese Communist Party successfully accomplished orderly leadership changes during its 15th Congress and the First Session of the Ninth National People's Congress. In its external relations, China continues to pursue a peaceful and independent foreign policy. China has shown great responsibility in dealing with the Asian financial

crisis and nuclear nonproliferation. These efforts have greatly elevated China's position in international affairs and in Japanese and
U.S. foreign relations.

China's recent success in improving its relations with the United
States has been significant. In October–November 1997, President
Jiang visited the United States, and the two countries concluded a
joint China-U.S. statement declaring their intention to form a constructive strategic partnership. In June–July 1998, President Clinton
returned the favor with an equally successful visit to China. This first
round of China-U.S. summits has advanced bilateral relations to a
higher level, symbolizing the renormalization of ties. The proposed
strategic partnership has served both as a framework for interaction
by both sides and a goal both can strive to achieve.

China-U.S. relations over the past few decades have focused on
four major issues: human rights, trade deficits, nuclear nonproliferation, and Taiwan. The two countries have made marked progress on
the nonproliferation issue, seen the Taiwan issue stabilize, played
down the human rights question, and continued to work at reducing
trade deficits. As long as no new, seriously damaging issues arise,
China and the United States should continue to move toward sustainable improvements in their relationship.

China has continued to single out the revised Guidelines for
U.S.-Japan Defense Cooperation for criticism, reprimanding Japan
in particular for including Taiwan in its coverage perimeters. China
has also been vigilant in watching for any indications that the Japanese government may try to change its policies toward Taiwan. This
may partially explain why the two countries have not yet established
a partnership per se.

Nevertheless, China has been working hard to improve its overall relations with Japan. Japan has become China's second largest
trading partner and source of foreign investment. China seeks to
maintain good relations with both Japan and the United States. President Jiang's visit has helped to define the nature of the Sino-Japanese
relationship at the start of the new century.

China has been acting responsibly in its handling of Asian regional
affairs. In the recent Asian financial crisis, China firmly committed
itself to nondevaluation of its currency, pledged support for Hong
Kong's currency peg to the U.S. dollar, and offered help to Thailand,

South Korea, and Indonesia through the International Monetary Fund. China's actions have cushioned the financial shock in the region and probably prevented another series of devaluations in Asia.

The improved China-U.S. relations have provided new depth to the trilateral relationship. By elevating the China-U.S. relationship to a "constructive strategic partnership," a better foundation has emerged for balanced relations among the three countries. While in Beijing, President Clinton called for a more active policy by the Japanese to stop further weakening of the yen and U.S. Treasury Secretary Robert Rubin suggested that Asians learn from Beijing instead of Tokyo on how to deal with the financial crisis.

Certainly, China has neither the intention nor the ability to replace the United States in playing a leadership role, either regionally or globally. As a developing country, China will not be on a par economically with Japan or the United States for a long time. Therefore, it would be unrealistic to predict that China would soon take over the role played by the United States in the Asia Pacific region. Trilateral cooperation thus seems the most desirable course for China.

AMERICA'S DECISIVE ROLE

In the foreseeable future, the United States will remain the only global superpower and, as such, it will play a decisive role in trilateral relations. Although the United States proclaims itself a global leader, its leadership admits that it must consult with the region's major powers in dealing with regional affairs. In the Asia Pacific region, it must consult, coordinate, and cooperate with both China and Japan.

The United States continues to stress its traditional bilateral alliances in the Asia Pacific region. Therefore, the Japan-U.S. alliance still outshines the China-U.S. relationship in significance. However, the United States has also found that its original expectation of making Japan-U.S. relations the cornerstone of its regional affairs no longer conforms to reality. Japan is obviously not ready to shoulder the heavy task of leadership that this implies. In addition, this expectation has already resulted in an unbalanced trilateral relationship.

Over the past few years, the United States has been trying to improve its relations with China, but its heavily weighted relationship with Japan has created more problems than it has solved. The revised Guidelines for U.S.-Japan Defense Cooperation have intensified suspicions between China on the one hand and the United States and Japan on the other. This imbalance has greatly curtailed the United States' ability to play a leading role in the Asia Pacific region.

In terms of trilateral cooperation, the United States continues to stress security concerns over other areas. The United States has expressed its desire that the three countries work together in the short term to ensure peace and stability on the Korean peninsula. Longer term, the United States wants to establish a mechanism for security cooperation. Currently, the United States is dissatisfied that ASEAN has taken the initiative on regional security matters through the ASEAN Regional Forum (ARF).

JAPAN'S UNCERTAIN ROLE

Despite its recent economic difficulties, Japan is still the world's second largest economy. Its economic weight is felt both regionally and globally. At the same time, Japan is making the transition from being solely an economic power to becoming a political and military presence as well. However, Japan is at a crossroads, facing the prospects of either maintaining its present international status or experiencing a downgraded position in global affairs.

In terms of trilateral relations, Japan occupies a complicated position. On the one hand, as an ally of the United States its relations with the United States have always been stronger than China's relationship with the United States. On the other hand, Japan is a distant second to the United States in terms of comprehensive national strength, and it faces an increasing challenge from China that even extends to economic might. Thus, Japan often worries that China and the United States may reach bilateral agreements at Japan's expense. Such often-bantered phrases as "Japan bashing," "Japan passing," and "Japan nothing" reflect the Japanese complex about its position vis-à-vis China.

Japan has limited political choices in trilateral relations. The present character of the trilateral relationship is to a great extent a product of history. A century of troubled relations between Japan and China still creates tensions because Japan has yet to fully acknowledge the mistakes it committed in the past. And the country's cold war alliance leaves Japan with little choice but to take the side of the United States when the latter experiences differences with China.

Furthermore, Japan has limited economic choices in the trilateral relationship. Japan was formerly the engine of economic growth in the Asia Pacific region, but since the bursting of its bubble economy and a slide into an officially confirmed recession, Japan's economic troubles have greatly limited its ability to act, either in regional or global affairs. For example, in the recent financial crisis Japan has been criticized for being irresponsible by letting the yen decline.

Japan is also weak on nuclear issues. Because of Japan's World War II history, it is difficult for Japan's Asian neighbors to allow Japan to play a leading role in nuclear matters. Japan did try to elevate its international status by proposing that the G-8 major industrial nations work together to help resolve the South Asian nuclear testing crisis. However, Japan was greatly disappointed when the United States and China jointly proposed that the five permanent members of the UN Security Council, which does not include Japan, play a leading role in nuclear matters.

CONCLUSION

Old ideas and ways of thinking do not easily fade away. Some strategists in the three countries still want to pit one nation against another, and some advocate trying to achieve national goals at the other nations' expense. Some do not want their nation to shoulder an equal share of the responsibilities yet seek benefits from this trilateral relationship. Other analysts express concern about the consequences of closer bilateral relations, such as the revised Guidelines for U.S.-Japan Defense Cooperation and President Clinton's recent visit to China.

All three countries should now try to adapt their previous mindsets to this new era by accepting new ideas, concepts, and ways of thinking. The concept that diplomacy should be a zero-sum game should gradually be replaced in the public's thinking by the more positive win-win theory, but it is much easier to speak of such changes than to implement them. The three partners can now seize a historic opportunity, as China, Japan, and the United States are all on good terms, thus creating a climate in which each party can win.

Fundamentally, the Taiwan issue is an internal matter between the Chinese on both sides of the Taiwan Strait. However, historically, the United States and Japan have been the two most important external actors. The Taiwanese authorities still look toward these two countries, and especially the United States, for help in bolstering their international standing. The mishandling of Taiwanese leader Lee Teng-hui's visit to the United States resulted in grave consequences for China-U.S. relations at the time. In the future, China, Japan, and the United States should continue to strengthen and improve a coordinated framework to deal with the international aspects of the Taiwan issue based on the "one China" principle.

It is still premature for the three to establish a formal system to manage their relations, but they should consult each other whenever necessary. They should also work harder to develop their bilateral and trilateral relations in a coordinated, well-balanced fashion. To achieve this, they should endeavor to achieve more transparency in both their diplomatic and political dealings.

The three countries should set realistic goals and cooperate to settle their differences step-by-step. In the immediate future, they should improve the financial stability of their government-level mechanisms, build up an effective second track for security cooperation, and press for broader, more intensive people-to-people exchanges.

The three countries would benefit from a stronger emphasis on mutual consultation, coordination, and cooperation. They should work more closely on the Korean peninsula issue, as its peace and stability are in their own interests. Specifically, they should continue to press for the Four-Party Talks and the continuation of the Korean Peninsula Energy Development Organization to stabilize the situation there. China, Japan, and the United States should conduct unofficial consultations as well, such as informal economic ministers' meetings at forums held by the Asian Development Bank, the Asia-Pacific Economic Cooperation forum, and ARF. The three countries should also keep each other informed concerning important events, such as President Jiang's visit to the United States and President Clinton's visit to China.

Because all three countries are major global powers, they should pay more attention to possible reactions concerning their activities and the repercussions of these activities on small and medium-sized countries in the region. Transparency in their activities is thus an important factor to ensure that each of these countries is informed about and involved in discussions of major regional issues.

Desirable as it is, a truly cooperative trilateral relationship is still an inspiration rather than a reality. We must be prepared for difficulties and occasional friction, for continued twists and turns in the relationship in the future. Especially, this relationship will be affected by many factors ranging from political differences to historical legacies, and the future will certainly bring new contradictions, conflicts, or even confrontations. All three countries should redouble their efforts to remove negative factors and build a constructive relationship with a view toward the new century.

CHAPTER III

Economics, Security, and Asian Stability after the Crash

Evan A. Feigenbaum

PITY THE ANALYST of East Asian security. The collapse of the Soviet Union destroyed much of the conceptual architecture that governed international security analysis from 1945 to 1991. But analysts of Asia Pacific security have had to contend with the demise of not one, but two, distinct cold wars. Each has left its distinct imprint on the shape of the present-day security challenges in the area. And whereas Europeans in the period since the collapse of Soviet power have sought to confront a security situation shaped by four decades of bipolarity, the division of the continent, and alliance patterns between two major blocs, Asia saw two successive phases of cold war–related strategic conflict in which shifting alliance patterns produced distinct security challenges.

The first of these two phases of the cold war in Asia lasted roughly from 1950 to 1960 and pitted the United States and its regional allies against a presumed Sino-Soviet bloc. Legacies of this initial phase include today's Taiwan and Korea problems and the security architecture of the Japan-U.S. alliance. After 1960–1961, in the wake of the Sino-Soviet split, new relationships (and new lines of cleavage) emerged to shape the security problems that confront Asia today.

These legacies include the China-U.S. and Sino-Japanese relationships and two related processes of economic integration—that of the Chinese economy into the region, and that of the Asia Pacific region into an increasingly interdependent and globally connected world of manufacturing, finance, and trade.

Although many security problems from both phases—particularly the Taiwan and Korea problems from the first—are still with us, all have changed fundamentally over the past decade.

For example, China and Taiwan continue to argue about their relationship and routinely trade rhetorical barbs. However, they also trade goods and exchange delegations to discuss common aspects of their economic and political future.

The Korean peninsula remains divided and a formal peace agreement still seems far off. Yet the two Koreas have conducted symbolically significant, if substantively inconclusive, government-to-government negotiations. A former dissident, once condemned to die, rules from the Blue House in Seoul, and a generational transition appears to be under way in Pyongyang. The founder of one of South Korea's leading *chaebol* conglomerates has traveled to North Korea in search of trade agreements. In part because of the failure of inter-Korean dialogue, the four major parties to the Korean War have undertaken several rounds of negotiations (sometimes at cross purposes). The United States and North Korea—antagonists for more than forty years—have negotiated a framework agreement on technical and political aspects of nuclear weapons and energy issues. The Korean Peninsula Energy Development Organization (KEDO), an administrative organization created out of that agreement, has been operational since August 1997.

In Southeast Asia, the United States and Vietnam, antagonists in Asia's last great hot war of global scope, have exchanged ambassadors. The Indochinese states—and even Myanmar—are full-fledged members of the Association of Southeast Asian Nations (ASEAN), with a seat in the region's councils of power and prestige.

Clearly, the conceptual architecture that has long governed the analysis of East Asian security has changed in potentially significant ways. And yet, if specific problem areas such as Taiwan, the Korean peninsula, and theater missile defense (TMD) have gained new urgency as truly regional, not simply cold war, problems, what once seemed to be purely economic and financial events of recent years have changed the playing field yet again.

The Promise of a Stable Future

Increasingly, the central problems in regional security dynamics seem connected to the recent economic and financial crises. To scholars of international relations this should come as little surprise. The connection between economics and security is among the oldest and most significant in theorizing about the global order. At various times in history, economic depression has exacerbated existing security tensions, while depression and plunging growth have fed military crises and the redrawing of the strategic balance.

Although narrowly defined security problems, such as TMD, are obviously critical to Asia's future, the region's present economic predicament bears direct consideration by those concerned with security and political relationships, not simply those worried about straightforward economic and financial issues.

This chapter details some analytical connections between economics and security in contemporary Northeast Asia and rejects analogies to earlier periods of global economic turbulence that have produced security tensions and led to international crises. Some recent writings on Northeast Asian security have emphasized potential conflicts and the notion that the region is "ripe for rivalry." If this were true, the economic crisis could be expected to make such tensions worse. History, after all, clearly shows that economic crisis can exacerbate strategic divisions. Indeed, there is a growing pessimism about Asia on this score among specialist and nonspecialist observers alike.

The central argument of this chapter, though, is that contemporary East Asia may fare far better than many pessimists expect. The security problems of the economic crisis are manageable in this case, in large part because the configuration of factors that have seemed to produce security tensions out of economic despair in the past do not exist in East Asia today.

HISTORICAL ECONOMIC-SECURITY LINK
NOT APPLICABLE

These factors have usually included the following:

- Prior existence of irredentist claims by major states on each other's territory. Irredentist claims exist in contemporary East Asia, but those by major states, such as China and Japan, on each other's territory do not concern core areas.
- Lack of an outside guarantor to encourage coordination and mediate regional tensions. Despite nativist and isolationist sentiment (and a debate about forward deployment of U.S. forces to the region that will likely grow more intense), the United States seems inclined to play the role of outside guarantor in contemporary East Asia in a way that it did not in Europe in the period between the two world wars. This may change over the long term, especially if Korean reunification becomes possible. But as Asia seeks to weather the current phase of economic crisis, the U.S. role as guarantor remains secure, providing a significant difference from earlier periods of economic and security tension in international history.
- States' pursuit of "beggar-thy-neighbor" resource and trade policies as a solution to their problems of economic crisis. East Asian states do not seem likely to adopt beggar-thy-neighbor economic strategies in response to the current financial crisis. Indeed, there appears to be a strong sense among Asian leaders that their national futures are linked to a stable regional and global future. An interwar-style grab for resources, particularly for those under the control of other states, does not seem likely as a solution to current and future problems.
- Absence of open global export markets, encouraging cycles of ever-greater protectionism by states facing economic collapse. Despite protectionist sentiment that may well grow if trade deficits balloon as U.S. exports to Asia taper off, U.S. markets are not likely to be closed to Asian exports. This will provide an important export outlet as the region seeks to weather its current difficulties and should reinforce the tendency to reject beggar-thy-neighbor policies.

Today's connection between economics and security is thus a comparatively hopeful one in many important respects. And when viewed in the context of changing China-Japan-U.S. relations, the prospect of security risks intensifying due to the current round of economic difficulty and its aftermath seems far less dire than some have predicted. Most important for the trilateral agenda, China-Japan-U.S. coordination on issues directly connected to the economic crisis may in fact yield a measure of coordination that could prove useful for handling security matters down the road.

U.S. ROLE CRUCIAL TO REGIONAL ORDER

In the short to medium term, the regional challenges for the United States are perhaps greater than for any power in East Asia. The United States must take an active leadership role in the region, and the forces of protectionism must be challenged head-on by advocates of openness in U.S. trade policy. At one level, this is a conventional position among observers of East Asian international relations. But it takes on new meaning and urgency when viewed specifically from the vantage point of historical analogues to today's economic crisis and the potential impact that such crises have had on security tensions throughout history. Asia has many advantages in this regard. However, two of the contemporary structural advantages outlined above depend, first and foremost, on continuing U.S. activism: its willingness to act as an outside guarantor within the region, and its commitment to markets that will remain open to Asian exports. A strategic and politically astute U.S. assertiveness—one that is sensitive to Asian nationalism and pride—is critical to medium-term regional stability. It is precisely the existence of these structural conditions that makes Asia's present economic and security experience so different—and so much more hopeful—than that of more unfortunate periods in international history.

This chapter has five sections. In the next, I consider how the economic crisis has forced a reexamination of several points of debate about the structure of power in East Asia. A third section considers the present against historical analogues along the four dimensions laid out above. The fourth section raises several problem areas related to the management of security relationships in Northeast Asia. The final section of the chapter asks whether the pursuit of realpolitik goals by the trilateral countries might have dangerous effects.

RECONSIDERING ASSUMPTIONS

In the wake of the economic crisis that has hit Asia full force in the last years of the 1990s, narrowly defined security issues of course remain critical throughout the region, especially among the trilateral countries of China, Japan, and the United States. Yet the economic crisis has had a variety of broader political implications that bear directly on some of the underlying assumptions that have long been made about security problems in the region. These implications include what the crisis means for various countries' external roles, their ability (and willingness) to exercise forward-looking leadership, and the ability of their leaders to focus on security problems given the short attention span of political decisionmakers preoccupied with economic matters.

On one level, the crisis thereby shows how much has changed during the past several years as a direct result of economic events in East Asia. First, this is because of the implications for attention to security problems and regional leadership. But most important, it is because—at a minimum—the financial crisis forces us to question some fundamental assumptions that have governed popular discussion of East Asian security and the China-Japan-U.S. relationship.

CHANGING POWER REALITIES

The first of these assumptions concerns the structure of power in the region and the changing relationship between relative power and the exercise of regional leadership. Prior to the economic crisis and throughout the 1990s, much popular and specialist opinion suggested a strong sense of "drift" in East Asia, particularly in relationships among China, Japan, and the United States. This found resonance in popular discussion, particularly in works by nonspecialists such as James Fallows (1994), but also in the work of some long-time specialists on Asian issues.

At its most essential, this drift was thought to reflect an inevitable time lag as new relative power realities reshaped relationships forged in a period when the structure of power in the region was different.

In this view, Japan, for example, was thought to be in the ascendant. Its economic and financial influence in Asia were gradually becoming a dominant feature of the regional political economy. A robust debate ensued over the possible evolution of a "yen bloc" in the Asian economies. Over time, some argued, this would require that Japanese political and perhaps even military influence eventually fall into line with new power realities derived from economic influence.

Thus the Japanese commentator Soeya Yoshihide (1998) and others argued that Japan has long possessed a complex dual identity within the Asian security environment. To most Japanese, he has suggested, the postwar experience essentially vitiated the country's role as an independent security actor in the region. However, "the realities of East Asian security . . . have not allowed Japan to enjoy this luxury entirely" (4). Thus, the country must inevitably take up some of the burdens of regional leadership for a series of reasons: geopolitical realities; Japan's latent great power potential; its ability to become a nuclear weapons state in a relatively short period of time; its advanced dual-use technology base; and the discrepancy between Japan's economic power and its weak political role in the region.

As Soeya and others predicted a Japanese political-military resurgence, the United States, though an obviously important economic and military force, seemed increasingly plagued over the 1990s by a distinct lack of political (and budgetary) will that would inevitably affect its leadership role in Asia. China, the third party in the trilateral interaction, was widely considered in pre-economic crisis analysis to be a non–status quo power whose ascendance, unlike Japan's (which was thought by many analysts to be conservative and status quo–preserving), might lead to a direct challenge to the prevailing East Asian order. Much was made, for example, of Chinese saber rattling in the South China Sea and the Taiwan Strait. Thus, despite considerable caution and sometimes out-and-out hostility to this "non–status quo" view from many specialists (see Yahuda 1993; Lampton 1997), many strategic analysts argued that China would prove a difficult partner in regional leadership (e.g., see Milhollin 1997). Even the more optimistic assessments nonetheless worried about the non–status quo aspects of Chinese policy.[1] In these views, much of China's foreign policy seemed based on probes designed to test the limits of others' resolve and to discover the limits of China's flexibility to maneuver in flaunting the status quo (Gregor 1996). One polar argument suggested that China's core strategic goal was simply to replace the other two regional leaders: an increasingly distracted United States, preoccupied at home and uninterested in the substance (as opposed to the rhetoric) of global leadership; and a Japan on the ascendant within its region but constrained by the United States, by its Peace Constitution, and by its limited resource base.[2]

By the end of 1998, the economic crisis had called into question many of these assumptions about the fundamental strategic balance in East Asia, at least in the short to medium term. The potentially "loose cannon" of Chinese policy and the notions of Japanese "ascendance" and U.S. "retreat" received prominent play in the popular debate, and by Fallows and others, in the period leading up to the crisis. Yet as the Asian financial system tottered on the brink of collapse, the crisis suddenly made the United States again appear robust within the region. Washington, or at least its Treasury and central bankers, took on the look of a leader whose actions were tempered by a certain caution, yet which, at the moment of highest crisis in 1998, seemed aggressive in filling a vacuum left because of limits to the International Monetary Fund (IMF) and the absence of leadership from other countries in the region.

By contrast, Japan's postcrisis turn inward—its preoccupation with domestic problems and the weakness of its government—raised new questions about the evolution of a broader political-military role for Japan in the Asia Pacific region. Indeed, Tokyo was roundly condemned within Asia for its failure to put its own economic house in order. Despite initial enthusiasm for a Japanese proposal to create an Asian IMF (a proposal that failed to receive U.S. support), the perception of comparative inertia remains widespread throughout Asia, and no wonder: market-opening issues remain secondary to budgetary matters; Japan's banking system continues to totter on the verge of insolvency, despite the announcement of measures designed to address elements of the problem;[3] and tax reduction, reflation, and a stimulation of consumer demand that might boost Asian exports to Japanese consumers remain uncertain items on the government's agenda. Indeed, if the Hashimoto government seemed lackluster on these issues, the Obuchi government, too, seems unwilling to tackle these problems through a concerted frontal assault.

Finally within Asia's great power triangle, China's response to the crisis was widely praised, including by the U.S. secretary of state, who held it up as a beacon of regional leadership (Albright 1998; Albright and Tang 1998). After nearly five years of sustained debate about China's inclination to take down the pillars of the regional status quo, this made China appear to be a somewhat more conservative power than many such arguments had initially implied. In fact, Beijing proved to be particularly active in promoting a regional response to the financial crisis, and raw Chinese self-interest converged with regional interest during 1998 to push Chinese policy in this direction. For example, Chinese efforts included moves to counter Taiwan's attempt to convert cash and comparative prosperity into political capital in Southeast Asia, where Taiwanese business made considerable inroads throughout the 1980s–1990s (e.g., see Feigenbaum 1995, 41–50). But whatever Beijing's motivations, China's response to the crisis was widely welcomed in a region hungry for a concrete demonstration of constructive Chinese leadership. It also bought Beijing considerable political capital. The Chinese government pledged US$1 billion to the Thai bailout. It promised to maintain the Hong Kong dollar peg. For the moment, at least, Beijing also continues to hold the line on the value of the renminbi.

AGENDA SETTING

A second assumption that governed much popular discussion about Asian security in the period leading up to the economic crisis was that the economic issues of the region were, in some sense, "settled," with security problems now likely to move to the forefront of the regional agenda. Analysis often contrasted Asia with Europe, where economic integration seemed to be promoting a new security order of peace and cooperation. In Asia, by contrast, security problems appeared to some commentators to belie a growing economic interdependence. Thus the breakdown of the cold war order and the evolution of a multipolar power structure could prove destabilizing, as it had throughout much of international history. A multipolar Asia, one important study therefore argued, was "ripe for rivalry," its prospects for peace far dimmer than in Europe, where integration was more intense and could check the distortionary effects of multipolarity. Almost inevitably, security would thus become a key focus of regional leaders and potentially undermine long-range progress toward cooperation and economic interdependence (see e.g., Friedberg 1993/1994 for an eloquent expression of the multipolar ripe-for-rivalry view). But in effect, the economic crisis had a curious impact here, pushing security problems off the top of the regional agenda as key security problems neither were solved nor disappeared.

Economic Crises and the Lessons of History[4]

A change of assumptions in these two areas ties directly into the implications of the financial crisis for Asian security: What are the prospects for the regional roles of the trilateral countries? What is the relationship between economics and security on Asia's agenda at a moment of great potential instability?

These questions are lent special appeal and urgency because there can be little doubt that Asia's current economic crisis remains dire. South Korea and Thailand appear well on the road to a recovery down the line. However, many financial analysts remain overwrought over the long-term prospects for Japan's main banking system. Harvard economist John Kenneth Galbraith (1998) has called today's global economic situation "the worst economic crisis of recent time, certainly the worst since World War II." Moreover, Galbraith implicitly suggests that renewed short-term confidence may ultimately prove false. Galbraith has offered explicit analogies to the late 1920s, comparing certain aspects of contemporary U.S. policy in the international economy to the "amiable indifference" of Calvin Coolidge and the false assurances about "sound fundamentals" of his successor, Herbert Hoover.

The depth of Asia's current crisis thus raises inevitable questions about the connection between economic crisis, resurgent nationalism, and security dilemmas. But it is the central argument of this chapter that the crisis will be unlikely to have negative implications for regional security.

There is, after all, a natural tendency to see in Asia's current crisis, as Galbraith does, analogies to earlier periods of global economic difficulty. This is particularly true of the interwar period when the connection between economic depression, domestic instability, rising nationalism, and security tensions had become particularly pronounced by the end of the 1930s. Not surprisingly, some have viewed Europe's past as a cautionary tale for contemporary East Asia. And this is especially the case if one accepts (as many do) the main premises of the ripe-for-rivalry argument—namely, that post–cold war East Asia, unlike post–cold war Europe, is fraught with unresolved security problems, old hostilities, latent tensions between China and Japan, rising nationalism, considerable potential for an arms race, an uncertain U.S. role in the region, and thus a drift toward true multipolarity.

In fact, however, the interwar case is instructive as a conceptual analogy *not* because it is analogous to contemporary East Asia but because it offers a useful comparative parallel of precisely what is likely to go right as East Asia weathers its current crisis. This cannot but be helpful as we consider the impact of fragile economies, weak governments, and domestic instability on security tensions in the region.

NATIONALISM AND IRREDENTISM

There are, first, fundamental differences between the two cases associated with irredentism and nationalism. The notion that economic collapse can feed virulent nationalism, especially when associated with fragile domestic politics, is an old one in international relations. It found special resonance in interwar Germany, where it became closely associated with the attempt to enforce irredentism claims.

It is not surprising, then, that serious analysts of East Asian security should have looked to outstanding territorial conflicts as a source of future tension. Among those analysts who are less subtle, the analogy to Germany is sometimes made directly, particularly the notion of a "rising" Germany hegemony that sought to challenge British, French, and American power in the 1930s–1940s. This has been used as an analytical framework for considering China's role in the emerging Asian future. However, more nuanced analysts, by contrast, tend to frame the problem simply in terms of rising Asian nationalism, particularly that of China, which does have a latent irredentist streak associated with the Senkaku/Diaoyu island chain in the East China Sea and the Spratly Islands in the South China Sea.

But the interwar European and present-day Asian cases are

different in some instructively fundamental ways. In Europe, core security problems not only preceded dire economic crisis but were virtually irreconcilable absent major changes in the security order and the redrawing of key borders. German demands and claims were, in many ways, mutually exclusive of those of France, Poland, and Czechoslovakia. Recent scholarship on interwar Germany has shown that even some of the most liberal voices in the Weimar state echoed National Socialist enthusiasm for irredentist claims on Austria. Meanwhile, German rearmament and a fundamentally altered security order were, for nearly all German political constituencies, the baseline conditions for a renewed German political role on the continent.

Much, then, is now made of China's irredentist claims to Taiwan, the Paracels, the Spratlys, and the Senkaku, and rightly so. Taiwan, in particular, presents perhaps the stickiest problem for future East Asian security. Yet none of the major powers of East Asia insist on core claims to each other's borders. And while the recent economic crisis has arrived on the heels of regional troubles on the Korean peninsula and in the Taiwan Strait, these by no means reflect the kind of fundamental security problems that forced the major powers of Europe to make claims on each other's territory and resources in decades past.

In short, Asian irredentism does exist. Yet it is of a decidedly more benign sort than we have seen in international history. Moreover, current Asian irredentism is on a smaller scale than in the past and seems restricted to more peripheral territorial claims. Only the Taiwan problem qualifies as an outstanding claim on a major chunk of territory. Yet no other great power's *own* territorial claims are affected by the dispute, and, in any case, there are reasons for optimism. After all, the dispute between China and the other major powers over Taiwan is not so much about the substance of China's claim as about the process through which that claim is to be arbitrated and resolved. Japan and the United States officially acknowledge the existence of a single China; even those in both countries who sympathize with the yearnings of some in Taiwan for greater local sovereignty do not deny that China has at least *some* historical basis to make a claim to ultimate sovereignty over the island. For Japan and the United States, then, at least in public and official business, China's threat of force—the issues of mechanics and process—is the key matter at stake, not the substance of the claim.

In this regard, it seems especially encouraging that the recent visit to China of Koo Chen-fu, chairman of Taiwan's Strait Exchange Foundation, has renewed the cross-strait dialogue. President Jiang Zemin's visit to Japan offers additional hopeful signs, and China and Japan seem disinclined to bring the Senkaku/Diaoyu problem to a head, whatever pressure latent domestic nationalism may exert. Indeed, as Richard Betts (1993/1994) has so aptly pointed out, for the first time in more than a century each bilateral relationship among the five dominant powers in the Asia Pacific region—China, India, Japan, Russia, and the United States—is peaceful.

Thus, while economic crisis has fed fundamental and irreconcilable security tensions between major powers in multipolar settings in the past, this hardly seems the case in contemporary East Asia. Irredentism remains focused at the margins, on peripheral claims. In fact, with the exception of Taiwan (which is, in many ways, sui generis as a territorial problem for Chinese leaders) and the Northern Territories (where Russo-Japanese conflict seems likely to be resolved at the bargaining table rather than by military means), the major powers seem to have found ways to dampen their most important disputes on outstanding territorial claims.

THE UNITED STATES AS
GUARANTOR OF LAST RESORT

The continuing existence of the United States as an ultimate guarantor of security order in the Asia Pacific region is also important when framed in the context of economic and diplomatic history. This does not, in any sense, imply that a specific or particular form of security order must remain in place over the longer term, including the present alliance and security structure in East Asia. But throughout international history, where no outside power has been in a position to interpose itself between regional powers with conflicting nationalist and security goals, tensions have grown.

This, then, provides a second comparative analogue to Europe between the wars, when the international economic system weathered its last great crisis but the United States all but withdrew from regional affairs, leaving European antagonists to work through fundamentally unworkable security problems without an outside guarantor. Today, despite isolationist sentiment in certain U.S. political circles, U.S. activism on financial and economic issues bridges the two-party divide and seems intact. And when framed in the context of past economic crises and security spirals, this provides much reason for optimism.

In fact, the greatest danger to U.S. input on economic matters seems to be the potential for (and U.S. fear of) a nationalistic backlash within the Asia Pacific region (see e.g. Snyder and Solomon 1998). However, the importance of a high-profile U.S. role seems clear to policy elites in the United States and is accepted—though not always in the same form—in Beijing, Tokyo, and Seoul. Clearly, then, the U.S. role as an outside guarantor lends an atmosphere of stability to regional affairs. Restraints on an independent security role for Japan remain important to China, and perhaps to others in the region. How difficult, then, would a post–Japan-U.S. alliance environment prove to be? Here, one sees the basis for major power accommodation on many security issues, but only so long as the U.S. role as a conventionally benign hegemonic power remains in place. As I have argued elsewhere, a large-scale U.S. military presence on the seas, in particular, keeps rivalries in check by discouraging the expansion of Japan's military power (Feigenbaum 1999a).

Although some regional elites may therefore wish for a reduced U.S. role in Asian security, restrictions on forward deployments, and a change in regional alliance and security relationships, that role seems more important than ever in a region burdened by economic crisis. For the moment, at least, the continued existence of that guarantee also sharply distinguishes present-day East Asia from earlier periods of history that have coupled economic crisis to latent security tension.

COORDINATION VERSUS BEGGAR-THY-NEIGHBOR MERCANTILISM

There is a third structural reason for optimism about the security implications of Asia's economic crisis. It concerns policy dynamics. One of history's most durable lessons is that when economic crises are solved through trade policies that seek relative gain at the expense of others, downward spirals of recrimination and political competition often ensue. Sometimes, as in interwar Europe, this takes the form of a forcible grab for the resources of rivals, and existing disputes over resource-rich regions in East Asia certainly bring this issue to the fore.

It is true that economic nationalism has long been a force in East Asia. The American political scientist Richard Samuels (1994), for example, has argued forcefully that "mercantile realism" remains a driving force in Japanese economic policy. In other work, I have also argued that relativistic, nationalist impulses once linked important aspects of Chinese economic policy directly to security concerns, particularly during the Mao Zedong era (1949–1976) (Feigenbaum 1999b). In both Japan and China, this has been particularly evident with respect to technology policy which, in both countries, focused on the acquisition of "strategic" technologies to enhance relative international standing and national economic competitiveness.[5]

Today, however, doses of mercantilism and nationalistic efforts to foster local technology are in no sense the conceptual equivalent of the beggar-thy-neighbor economic nationalism that vitiated efforts at regional policy coordination in earlier periods of international history. Unlike interwar Europe, where protectionism intensified in response to the economic crisis, today's Asian crisis seems to have reinforced elements of a "rise together, fall together" mentality. Robert B. Zoellick (1998), a former U.S. state and treasury department official, has noted that efforts at regional and global trade liberalization have entered a period of distress. The Mercosur countries of South America (Argentina, Brazil, Paraguay, and Uruguay), for example, have increased common external tariffs in response to Latin America's economic crisis by 25 percent (from 12 to 15 percent). And, of course, competitive currency devaluations might lead to intensified competition and political recrimination.

Still, while pledges to implement World Trade Organization financial services and sectoral liberalization agreements have been put on hold, governmental responses to the crisis thus far provide evidence that Asians are unlikely to choose market closure as a long-term solution to current problems. For example, South Korea's government, in particular, has begun to make painful, yet promising, changes to its domestic economic structure. Recent steps by the Thai government also mirror a domestic-oriented approach to economic reflation. In Japan, the Obuchi government, however tentatively, has made domestic restructuring, not externally oriented protection, the cornerstone of its economic program.

There is little evidence, then, that resource constraints are viewed by Asian leaders as a significant factor inhibiting continued growth. And particularly because Asian irredentism is focused on peripheral territories, not core resource-producing areas (as was the case with Japan's grab of Manchuria and Southeast Asia in the 1930s and 1940s), the prospects for cooperative resource development also seem promising. While the Spratly issue, of course, remains difficult, China has made noises about joint development. Moreover, Chinese claims to the Spratlys, however rigorously they are enforced, may say more about rigid Chinese sovereignty values than about broader strategic trends and are not necessarily inconsistent with the U.S. role in Asia's sea-lanes (Feigenbaum 1999a). The Spratlys also offer no solution to the economic problems that the Chinese and other Asian governments will face in coming years.

EXPORTS AND POLITICAL PRESSURES ON THE ROAD BACK TO PROSPERITY

One final cause for optimism is the continuing commitment of U.S. leaders of both political parties to open markets. This economic role directly parallels the U.S. political role as a guarantor of regional security. It has become increasingly clear since mid-1998 that tension in this area is likely to grow in the years ahead. Manufacturing sectors that depend heavily on exports to Asia will likely see dips in earnings. Trade deficits may balloon. There will be pressure on the Federal Reserve to nudge up interest rates. There is also considerable potential for a political backlash within the United States. In short, the notion of a free ride for troubled Asian economies to export their way back to prosperity will be unpopular in the United States. And in any case, the United States cannot stand alone as the source of Asian recovery, for as Snyder and Solomon (1998) have noted, multiple "tugboats," including reflation of the Japanese economy and market liberalization in Japan, are necessary.

Ultimately, however, recovery in Asia is as important to the United States as it is to East Asia. The highest-growth U.S. manufacturing sectors, including software, mainframes and other computer hardware, and telecommunications systems, depend on it. Thousands of jobs are at stake. This provides a fourth structural reason for optimism about the current crisis: Whereas protectionist spirals accompanied past global economic crises and often produced negative security implications, the commitment of U.S. political and business leaders to open markets seems firm, despite the political backlash that will surely accompany U.S. support for Asian exporters.

Security Management

Four variables, then, have been among the most important in determining whether past global economic crises have intertwined with nationalism and political factors to produce negative security effects. Yet in Asia, the presence of positive signs in all four variables sharply distinguishes the present crisis from that of the 1930s and from smaller shocks. Despite these reasons for hope at a structural level, a number of important challenges nonetheless exist at the level of day-to-day policy making in the management of regional security relationships.

UNRESOLVED SECURITY PROBLEMS

Many of the security problems that lie at the center of the ripe-for-rivalry argument remain unresolved, even as the agenda seems to have shifted away from security to pressing economic matters.

PROBLEMS OF STATESMANSHIP

The scale of Asia's economic problems is enormous and appears increasingly unlikely to be solved absent significant domestic change, perhaps involving much suffering and financial pain for individual citizens (Japan Center for International Exchange and Institute of Southeast Asian Studies 1999). We have already seen this in South Korea and Indonesia, and we seem increasingly certain to see it in

Japan as well. In this context, great potential suffering, coupled with democratization, loud domestic political opinion, and the increased effectiveness of domestic lobbyists pressuring their respective governments, will surely make statesmanship far more difficult for regional leaders.

The difficulties facing South Korea's Kim Dae Jung exemplify the contradiction between statesmanlike risks on security matters (Kim's "Sunshine Policy" toward the North) and the need to focus on purely domestic problems. Such concerns will not only distract leaders' attention but also make compromise on security issues more difficult for three reasons:

- Any compromise that involves trade-offs affecting domestic prosperity and welfare will be a difficult sell.
- Governments have been weakened.
- Cross-cutting bureaucratic and other pressures will surely increase, giving leaders and governments less room to maneuver within their domestic political contexts.

INSTABILITY AND MISPERCEPTION

Trilateral relationships can be extremely problematic in international politics. Funabashi Yōichi (1998), in particular, has raised the issues of mistrust and misperception in interactions involving three, instead of two, parties, where all look askance at one another and each side worries about potential collusion between the remaining two.

But if this is true, then trust—and eventually institutionalized trust through transparency, dialogue, confidence-building measures (CBMs), and preventive defense mechanisms—becomes that much more important.[6] The Jiang-Clinton exchange of summits augurs well for longer-term China-U.S. coordination, despite the Belgrade embassy bombing and other sources of short-term conflict. Jiang's visit to Japan also bodes especially well for Sino-Japanese confidence-building, particularly because the Sino-Japanese leg of the triangle has long seemed to be the weakest. But what happens to the prospects for this type of trust when the environment puts as much pressure on leaders, governments, lobby groups, and so on, as is likely to result from the fallout related to the economic crisis?

RELATIONSHIPS AS ISSUES
RATHER THAN FRAMEWORKS

During the cold war, moreover, China-U.S., Japan-U.S., and Sino-Japanese interactions functioned as frameworks within which the parties tackled greater security challenges. Increasingly, however, these interactions have ceased to be a part of a larger strategic context but seem, in some sense, themselves to have become the strategic issue at stake. Thus, when U.S. opinion makers ask, "What should our relationship with China be?" some seem disposed to frame the issue as a strategic dilemma in and of itself. This is a sharp break with the past. For if the mere idea of a relationship is presented as a strategic issue, then the fundamental premises of most CBMs, cooperative security schemes, and preventive defense mechanisms must come into question as well.

Advocates of CBMs generally argue that the mere existence of relationships can be an important stabilizing force in international politics. Relationships create a reservoir of trust, while providing avenues for coordination and cooperation. Various forms of CBMs thereby help to control for misperception by building a legacy of collaboration on which leaders can draw in the event of future disputes.

This offers an analytic window into why it may be dangerous if post–cold war decisionmakers on the three sides of the China-Japan-U.S. triangle, particularly those in the United States, should come to view relationships not as intrinsically important but, rather, as involving strategic trade-offs from among which leaders must choose. All relationships have a clear strategic dimension. But if, as in some recent U.S. opinion, the very *premises* of a relationship come into question, the prospects for CBMs and cooperative security inevitably deteriorate. The China-U.S. relationship has become particularly fragile in this regard. As a result of three major political debates of 1998–1999—one related to space launch technology, the second to campaign finance, and the third to allegations of espionage at U.S. nuclear weapons laboratories—many of the rationales that have underpinned two decades of broad-ranging Sino-American cooperation have come under attack in U.S. political debate. Indeed, much recent U.S. commentary, particularly in the media and on Capitol Hill, has none-too-subtly implied that these events violate the very principles that were originally offered as the framework to justify bilateral coordination: mutual interest and a growing trust between the two countries. On the Chinese side, meanwhile, perceptions of latent U.S. hostility, particularly in the wake of the Belgrade embassy bombing, have increasingly placed the relationship with the United States under strain in Beijing's political circles. To those who advocate CBMs as an avenue to coordination, such an atmosphere is unhealthy, not least because the relationship itself, not simply the issues that divide the two sides, becomes the political issue under debate.

TAIWAN, KOREA, AND TMD

All of the above policy challenges, particularly the problems of misperception and statesmanship, carry a variety of implications for how specific issues, such as Taiwan, TMD, and achieving peace and stability on the Korean peninsula, are likely to be managed by the trilateral countries. Certainly, such cautions and constraints bear directly on the likelihood of their being managed trilaterally, as opposed to bilaterally.

In fact, the triangle hangs like a shadow over most bilateral interaction among the three major Asia Pacific powers. Thus, whereas China and the United States may talk bilaterally about Taiwan, the Guidelines for U.S.-Japan Defense Cooperation touch all aspects of bilateral coordination on the issue. Chinese analysts have expressed concern about the implications of the guidelines for Taiwan (Wang 1998). Meanwhile, officials in Tokyo and Washington have been ambiguous about what the new framework may mean in concrete terms for the Taiwan problem in the event that hostilities break out.

This essentially triangular dimension—the fact that few issues can truly be treated in a purely bilateral context in Northeast Asia—also shapes Korean issues, and especially the matter of TMD. Thus, it is not surprising that it has become difficult for Japan and the United States to discuss TMD vis-à-vis North Korea in a purely bilateral context without raising hackles on the Chinese side.

REALPOLITIK AND LONG-TERM INSTABILITY

For all of these reasons, the political stakes of the Asian economic crisis for all three trilateral partners, as for all countries in the region, are high. At the same time, those stakes have security implications, not merely implications for economic prosperity and continued growth, because they have made cooperation critical. The structural dimensions of the economic-security linkage in East Asia may provide reason for optimism. The crisis may also provide new opportunities and avenues for bilateral, trilateral, and multilateral coordination in Asia, as well as an important basis for confronting problems not directly related to the crisis down the road. However, two fundamental questions cut directly to security and political concerns at the structural level: How will the Sino-Japanese relationship evolve as Japan battles to overcome the distortionary effects of economic decay? And what does a China-U.S. "strategic partnership," whatever form it may take, mean for Japan?

Both questions are the logical outgrowth of realpolitik-type thinking, for as Wang Jisi has noted, "U.S. officials and analysts point to the potential rivalry between Japan and China" (1998, 24), and many Chinese and Japanese analysts point to the problem as well (see e.g. Christensen 1999). Mistrust remains pervasive in Sino-Japanese relations, despite three decades of extraordinary progress between Asia's two great indigenous powers. Greater power competition has been a stable feature of international relations for many centuries. Thus, it is important to ask whether, as Snyder and Solomon contend, "Asia's financial crisis may mark a shift in relative long-term influence in favor of China at the expense of Japan" (1998, 1). If so, then those who believe that China and Japan are destined to renew their strategic competition of the early part of this century may ask: Are there those on one or the other side who might try to exploit the weaknesses introduced by the economic crisis? How, then, might this crosscut Funabashi's (1998) suggestion that triangular relationships reinforce suspicions about collusion between two parties at the expense of the third?

TRILATERAL INTERACTION: A STRUGGLING JAPAN, A DYNAMIC CHINA-U.S. RELATIONSHIP

Few strategic analysts are likely to disagree that Asia's great powers succeed best when they hang together. Yet, as Thomas Christensen (1999) has argued, many Chinese remain deeply troubled by the

emergence of Japanese power, while a strong ambivalence charac-
terizes Japanese perceptions of China. As Christensen has noted,
the issue of Sino-Japanese competition, however delicate, is lent special weight by historical rivalries and the structural realities of great
power conflict through East Asian history. And it may now have
become more acute because of recent economic events.

It is no longer inconceivable that economic restructuring could
hobble Japan financially, create problems for its once rapidly expanding economic role in the region, and make it less likely to evolve
into the aggressive, forward- and outward-looking power that once
seemed likely to be thrust onto the stage as a genuine regional leader.
On some level, serious analysis in the wake of the financial crisis must
recognize that, when viewed through the historical and conceptual
lens of great power competition, Japanese weakness could provide
certain strategic opportunities to Chinese political constituencies that
regard the potential expansion of Japanese military power with concern. A weaker yen may pose problems for Chinese economic policymakers, and Beijing has made its unhappiness with Japanese fiscal
policy known to Tokyo. But one cannot help but wonder whether
Chinese security constituencies concerned about the expansion of
Japanese defense roles in Asia might not view a "weakening" of Japan
in this way as favorable to China's own strategic prospects.

This takes on special resonance in the complex geometry of trilateral interaction because the trilateral relationship has long been
asymmetrical, with two sides of the triangle (Japan and the United
States) more powerful and prosperous (and more closely tied by
bonds of interdependence and trust) than the third. Might the economic crisis in some way lay a foundation that will ultimately alter
these asymmetries? More important, will coordination over matters
related to the crisis—the widespread suggestion over the past year of
U.S. "pleasure" with China's monetary "statesmanship," contrasted
with frustration over Japan's "paralysis"—change the dynamic
through which the sides of the triangle, particularly China and the
United States, interact?

This discussion accelerated in 1998, in large part because of the
complex reaction in Japan to President Clinton's China trip, coupled
with Secretary of State Madeleine Albright's trip of reassurance to
Tokyo in the wake of the visit. Those events made clear that there is

a strong element of ambivalence in Tokyo about what closer China-U.S. ties mean for Japan. Some Japanese analysts clearly regard Japan's strategic position in the triangle as having been undercut by a new phase of closer China-U.S. bilateralism.

If one believes, then, that some Chinese policymakers might regard a hobbled Japan as strengthening China's strategic position in the region, East Asia is likely to experience a vastly different trilateral dynamic than might be the case if Japan deals smoothly with its current crises and rapidly sets itself back on course. This dynamic of strategic competition demonstrates clearly why institutionalized trust and the avoidance of misperception are so important to regional stability. Future strategic relationships among great powers are likely to mix aspects of cooperation and rivalry (see e.g. Feigenbaum 1999a). Thus, three strong, secure, and assertive trilateral powers—potential rivals in some areas, but strategic partners in the maintenance of Asian economic and political stability—best reflect the interests of all three countries and the Asia Pacific region at large.

THE UNITED STATES AND REGIONAL COORDINATION

Above all, the concerns voiced by China and Japan make clear just how important it has become that the trilateral countries view their relations as partnerships, with stability in each bilateral interaction reinforcing the stability of the triangle as a whole. While deepening its relations with China, the United States must reassure Japan. The Sino-Japanese relationship, in particular, has become the critical leg of the triangle.

In recent years, there has been a growing recognition in all three capitals that regional problems, whether economic or security-oriented, reflect the challenges of a shared future. This does not imply that all interests are commonly shared, simply that stability is important to all. Yet stability—a shared interest—becomes easier to achieve when actors recognize their common stake in its maintenance. This is the most important political and strategic lesson of the Asian financial crisis, which has shown decisively just how much of the region's economic future is shared. For two decades, sustained economic growth has been the most important goal of all major Asian countries, including post-Mao China.

This explicit recognition of the need to share in a coordinated regional response to today's economic crisis is thus particularly encouraging. Tomorrow's Asia Pacific region will be shaped, in large part, by how countries face down this present challenge. Cooperation amid potential strategic rivalry is never easy. Many analysts have pointed to the problems that Asian leaders will have to confront to sustain coordination in the face of domestic political pressure, threats to regime legitimacy, and painful economic restructuring choices that may further undermine popular support. The most poignant example of sustained intraregional cooperation on political matters—the ASEAN model—has come in for harsh scrutiny as the crisis has intensified.

Yet if, as this chapter contends, the future seems brighter than pessimists predict, it is because important structural conditions in place in today's Asia were absent from earlier regional and global economic crises. This not only provides a historical baseline for optimism. It also presents a strategic opportunity. Responding constructively and cooperatively to the challenges of a new era requires that partners overcome all of the reasons for pessimism to which observers of Asian security routinely point:

- Reservoirs of distrust.
- Problems of misperception.
- The reality of conflicting interests in some important areas.
- A future that will include Korean reunification and thus require adjustments to the regional structure, especially with respect to the U.S. military role.

The current crisis should make clear even to those Asians who actively seek a reduced U.S. role in the region that a medium-term continuation of that role has become vital to the very stability that will ultimately make such change possible. The United States plays the critical role in guaranteeing the structural conditions that make today's situation hopeful. On two levels—the exercise of strategic leadership, and a commitment to market openness—the U.S. role is simply indispensable to prevent the economic crisis from feeding security problems.

This is not to argue that any particular political or security order must remain in place over the long term to guarantee stability. It is not necessarily a recipe for a permanent U.S. forward presence.

Someday, Korea will be reunified. Will a role for forward-deployed U.S. forces on the peninsula then be sustainable? Chinese diplomats have expressed their sensitivity to some of the rationales offered for the continuation of a Japan-U.S. alliance forged during a very different era. Tokyo and Washington must both make a more compelling case to Chinese leaders that is sensitive to their concerns.

Most important, then, acknowledging U.S. "leadership" implies that Washington is a genuine partner—a constituent member of a region whose problems should be shared. This is neither a new nor an especially surprising conclusion. Fighting the economic crisis required partnership, and partnership requires coordination. Under a positive set of structural conditions that is likely to prevent economic problems from feeding security concerns, coordination on pressing economic matters, especially among China, Japan, and the United States, may ultimately create useful channels for partnership on strategically sensitive questions.

Notes

1. See, for instance, Fareed Zakaria (1997), who argues for a view of Chinese strength, coupled with a prediction of a fundamentally conservative Chinese foreign policy. China is not a "rogue," Zakaria argues, because it largely lacks the resources to be one. The region should relax, he seems to argue, but must also be on its guard. Fuel for the more extreme arguments about Chinese intentions came from a variety of events and statements. A good example concerns Sino-Russian cooperation, the goals and outlines of which still remain murky and which many suspect amount mostly to rhetorical posturing. On China and Russia, see for example Gordon (1997).

2. The polar argument, which has been discredited among most specialist and popular audiences alike, has been made by Bernstein and Munro (1997). A good rejoinder is Nathan and Ross (1997). However, many analysts who view China's ascendance more conservatively than Bernstein and Munro nonetheless predict potential challenges to the existing order as a key Chinese goal. See, for instance, Christensen (1996). See also the debate between Roy (1994) and Gallagher (1994).

3. For a sense of how dramatic this problem is, one need only consider the story of Japan Leasing Corporation, a subsidiary of the Long-Term Credit Bank of Japan, which is itself in trouble. By the end of September 1998, Japan Leasing had gone under with more than US$16 billion in debt. The Japanese government's efforts to address the banking crisis have thus far focused on how to guarantee deposits without bailing out the banks per se. The refusal to guarantee Japan Leasing's debt may be a recurring story in Japan's financial crisis.

4. I am grateful to Francis Gavin for discussion of the major points in this section.

5. On Japanese "technonationalism" and "mercantile realism," see Samuels (1994) and Heginbotham and Samuels (1998). On China, see Feigenbaum (1999b, 1999c).

6. Much has been written about this issue. The most eloquent treatment, which is also somewhat pessimistic, is by the Canadian scholar Paul Evans. See, for example, Evans (1993; 1994). On some of the reasons why transparency and regional security dialogue are important, see the discussion in the context of arms race concerns by Ball (1993/1994). One positive byproduct of Asia's otherwise unfortunate economic crisis may be the effect that it will inevitably have on acquisition budgets and the potential for regional arms races. The title of Ball's pre-economic crisis article, "Arms and Affluence," is, in this sense, particularly poignant: Strapped for cash, most Asian governments will find it difficult to pursue expensive force modernization programs. Thus, for the moment the problems of the crisis, unfortunate as they are for regional leaders, may vitiate some of the concern from three to five years ago about the possibility of a regional arms race.

BIBLIOGRAPHY

Albright, Madeleine. 1998. "Remarks to Business Representatives." <http://www.state.gov/www/current/debate/chinasph.html> (Beijing, 30 April), Web site accessed November 1998.

Albright, Madeleine, and Tang Jiaxuan. 1998. "Joint Remarks." <http://www.state.gov/www/current/debate/chinasph.html> (Washington, D.C., 29 September), Web site accessed November 1998.

Ball, Desmond. 1993/1994. "Arms and Affluence: Military Acquisitions in the Asia-Pacific Region." *International Security* 18(3): 78–112.

Bernstein, Richard, and H. Ross Munro. 1997. *The Coming Conflict with China.* New York: Alfred Knopf.

Betts, Richard K. 1993/1994. "Wealth, Power, and Instability: East Asia and the United States after the Cold War." *International Security* 18(3): 34–77.

Christensen, Thomas J. 1996. "Chinese Realpolitik." *Foreign Affairs* 75(5): 37–52.

———. 1999. "China, the U.S.-Japan Alliance, and the Security Dilemma in East Asia." *International Security* 23(4): 49–80.

Evans, Paul M. 1993. *The Agenda for Cooperative Security in the North Pacific.* North York, Ont.: North Pacific Cooperative Security Dialogue, Research Program.

———. 1994. *The Council for Security Cooperation in the Asia Pacific: Context and Prospects.* North York, Ont.: Canadian Consortium on Asia Pacific Security.

Fallows, James. 1994. *Looking at the Sun: The Rise of the New East Asian Economic and Political System.* New York: Pantheon.

Feigenbaum, Evan A. 1995. *Change in Taiwan and Potential Adversity in the Strait.* Santa Monica, Calif.: RAND Corp.

———. 1999a. "China's Military Posture and the New Economic Geopolitics." *Survival* 41(2): 71–88.

———. 1999b. "Soldiers, Weapons, and Chinese Development Strategy: The Mao Era Military in China's Economic and Institutional Debate." *China Quarterly* 158: 285–313.

———. 1999c. "Who's Behind China's High-Technology 'Revolution'? How Bomb Makers Remade Beijing's Priorities, Policies, and Institutions." *International Security* 24(1).

Friedberg, Aaron L. 1993/1994. "Ripe for Rivalry: Prospects for Peace in a Multipolar Asia." *International Security* 18(3): 5–33.

Funabashi Yōichi. 1998. "Thinking Trilaterally." In Morton Abramowitz, Funabashi Yōichi, and Wang Jisi. *China-Japan-U.S.: Managing the Trilateral Relationship.* Tokyo and New York: Japan Center for International Exchange.

Galbraith, John Kenneth. 1998. "Evading the Obvious." *New York Times* (12 October): Section A.

Gallagher, Michael. 1994. "China's Illusory Threat to the South China Sea." *International Security* 19(1): 169–194.

Gordon, Michael. 1997. "Russia and China Say They'll Work Together to Limit U.S. Power." *New York Times* (24 April): Section A.

Gregor, A. James. 1996. "China, the United States, and Security Policy in East Asia." *Parameters* 26(2): 92–101.

Heginbotham, Eric, and Richard J. Samuels. 1998. "Mercantile Realism and Japanese Foreign Policy." *International Security* 22(4): 171–203.

Japan Center for International Exchange and Institute of Southeast Asian Studies (1999). *The Asian Crisis and Human Security: An Intellectual Dialogue on Building Asia's Tomorrow.* Tokyo and Singapore: Japan Center for International Exchange and Institute of Southeast Asian Studies.

Lampton, David M. 1997. "A Growing China in a Shrinking World: Beijing and the Global Order." In Ezra F. Vogel, ed. *Living with China: U.S.-China Relations in the Twenty-First Century.* New York: W. W. Norton.

Lee Jong Won. 1998. "Recent Developments in the Korean Peninsula and the China-Japan-U.S. Trilateral Relationship." Conference presentation, Japan Center for International Exchange (July 1998, Washington, D.C.).

Milhollin, Gary. 1997. "China Cheats (What a Surprise!)." *New York Times* (24 April): Section A.

Nathan, Andrew J., and Robert S. Ross. 1997. *The Great Wall and the Empty Fortress: China's Search for Security.* New York: W. W. Norton.

Roy, Denny. 1994. "Hegemon on the Horizon? China's Threat to East Asian Security." *International Security* 19(1): 149–168.

Samuels, Richard J. 1994. *Rich Nation, Strong Army: National Security and the Technological Transformation of Japan.* Ithaca, N.Y.: Cornell University Press.

Snyder, Scott, and Richard H. Solomon. 1998. "Beyond the Asian Financial Crisis: Challenges and Opportunities for U.S. Leadership." U.S. Institute of Peace Special Report. Washington, D.C.: U.S. Institute of Peace.

Soeya Yoshihide. 1998. *Japan's Dual Identity and the U.S.-Japan Alliance.* Stanford, Calif.: Asia/Pacific Research Center, Stanford University.

Wang Jisi. 1998. "Building a Constructive Relationship." In Morton Abramowitz, Funabashi Yōichi, and Wang Jisi. *China-Japan-U.S.: Managing the Trilateral Relationship.* Tokyo and New York: Japan Center for International Exchange.

Yahuda, Michael. 1993. "China: Will It Strengthen or Weaken the Region?" In T. B. Millar and James Walter, eds. *Asian Pacific Security after the Cold War.* Canberra: Australian National University Press.

Zakaria, Fareed. 1997. "Let's Get Our Superpowers Straight." *New York Times* (26 March): Section A, 19.

Zoellick, Robert B. 1998. *The Political and Security Implications of the East Asian Crisis.* National Bureau of Asian Research Report 9(4). Washington, D.C.: National Bureau of Asian Research.

CHAPTER IV

The Asian Financial Crisis and the Trilateral Relationship

Watanabe Kōji

THE ASIAN FINANCIAL CRISIS, which began in July 1997 in Thailand and now affects the whole of East Asia, has brought into relief three popular national images: China as the good guy, Japan as the bad guy, and the United States as the smugly prosperous arbiter of events. These characterizations were amplified by President Bill Clinton's historic visit to China. To the extent that these images contribute to improved relations between China and the United States, Japan should welcome them. But it would be disturbing—not only for Japan but also for East Asia as a whole—if such an improvement in China-U.S. relations was to take place at the cost of a deterioration in Japan-U.S. relations.

CHINA SPURNS DEVALUATION

China has behaved commendably so far in the face of the Asian financial crisis, and there is no reason to believe that China will act differently in the future, given the determination expressed by Chinese leaders, particularly Premier Zhu Rongji. As U.S. Treasury Secretary Robert Rubin said recently, "One continues to be impressed by the vision of [China's] leaders and by the understanding they express of the issues they face. They continue to express a determination to move along at a good pace."

This determination on the part of the Chinese government in executing policies has two components. First, despite the undeniable effect on China of the Asian financial crisis, China is committed to pursuing its more open, pro-reform policies, particularly the three-pronged reforms of state-owned enterprises, financial institutions, and government administration. Second, China has said that it will not devalue the renminbi, an expression of determination greatly appreciated by Japan and other countries around the world.

It is important to note, however, that the Chinese decision not to devalue the renminbi was made not primarily in the interest of the East Asian and world economies but, more significantly, in China's own interest. What is remarkable is the skill with which the Chinese presented the country's determination not to devalue its currency as a display of their strongly felt sense of responsibility as a great Asian power and the enthusiasm with which Americans praised it, implicitly contrasting China's statesmanship with what they decry as the "too little, too late" behavior of Japanese leaders.

Indeed, devaluation is neither necessary nor appropriate for China at this juncture. First, China's trade surplus is huge, amounting to more than US$40 billion in 1997. The surplus for January–May of 1998 was US$22 billion, a substantial increase over the same period in 1997. Second, China is a net importer of capital, with foreign exchange reserves of US$140 billion, the second largest figure after Japan. Third, the effects of devaluation would not adequately serve the intended purpose because more than 50 percent of China's exports are in the form of processed trade and, significantly, a major Chinese export category, textile products, would not accrue substantial benefits from devaluation because it is subject to import quotas in virtually all developed countries, with the exception of Japan. Fourth, devaluation would have a negative effect because Chinese foreign currency denominated debt stands at US$130 billion, with an annual repayment obligation of US$32.4 billion. Finally, should China perceive the need to maintain export price competitiveness vis-à-vis devalued currencies, which could be a real possibility, the government would most likely increase the amount and expand the coverage of its domestic tax rebate for exporters, from 9 percent of the value of textile exports to 17 percent of all export items.

Furthermore, the Chinese yuan is not fully convertible, and therefore China can maintain a stable currency much more easily than other countries, should it so desire. For example, Chinese nationals in China cannot buy foreign currencies due to tight restrictions on foreign exchange capital transactions. Therefore, it is relatively easy for the Chinese authorities to fend off speculative short-term capital movements.

This does not imply, of course, that the Chinese need not be concerned about the Japanese economy and the value of the yen. Concern on the part of China is legitimate and, in a sense, appreciated. Japan should value the role allegedly played by the Chinese in persuading the reluctant Americans to join with Japan to intervene in the currency markets to stabilize the yen on June 17, 1998. If the yen had tumbled further, the consequences would have been most serious for the regional economy. China itself, notwithstanding the above arguments, would also have suffered enormously, particularly through Hong Kong.

Japan should also welcome the determination of China's leaders to move forward regarding the three-pronged reforms of state-owned enterprises, financial institutions, and government administration. However, reform in China has just begun, as the result of decisions made at the 15th Party Congress in the autumn of 1997, and some of the problems China is going to confront will be as difficult as, if not more difficult than, those that Japan now faces. In fact, the types of serious challenges entailed by reform of China's financial institutions look strikingly similar to those facing Japanese banks. Japan is prepared to share its hard-won experience and to extend whatever assistance its neighbor requests to support Chinese efforts to carry out reform because the success of these efforts will be important to the future well-being of the whole region, including Japan.

Japan does not claim to be the good guy in the ongoing financial crisis. Its performance has not been commendable. The criticism that Japan has been doing "too little, too late" may be well deserved —but only to a certain extent. It is going too far to criticize Japan as an irresponsible player in the unfolding drama of the Asian financial crisis, particularly in juxtaposition with China.

Japan is hardly the cause of the Asian financial crisis. Certainly, Japan played a crucial role in making East Asia a centerpiece of dynamic growth in the 1970s and 1980s through its direct investment, transfer of technology, and official development assistance. However, Japan can hardly be blamed for being a model for the type of growth that led to the current crisis.

More important, Japan has suffered a prolonged period of stagnation since 1992, when the economic bubble that had prevailed since the mid-1980s finally burst. Even so, many Japanese have assumed that somehow the economy would return to its old growth patterns more or less automatically, but that assumption has turned out to be tragically inaccurate. Because of Japan's remarkable economic success, it took several years to acknowledge reality and to recognize that, as Keidanren (Japan Federation of Economic Organizations) declared in its 1997–1998 annual report, "the social and economic systems that created [Japan's] prosperity are now obsolete" and that "Japan will not be able to cope with the changing circumstances inside and outside the country, such as the competition emerging from the global marketplace and the rapid aging of its population." It has taken so long to realize that the system was not functioning precisely because it had worked so well in the past in propelling Japan to its current status as the world's second largest economy.

It just so happened that the Asian financial crisis started in the latter part of 1997, just as Japan found itself in the midst of its most serious policy dilemma in decades. Forced to choose between adopting a policy aimed at reforming the fiscal deficit on the one hand and a policy of sustaining growth on the other, the government decided in the early months of 1997 that the forces of recovery were strong enough to withstand tight fiscal policy—a judgment that has since proved wrong. But had there been no Asian financial crisis or bankruptcies of major Japanese commercial banks and brokerage firms during the autumn of 1997, revealing the dire fragility of the financial sector, the tight fiscal policy adopted in 1997 might not have resulted in a recession. In such a situation, the economy instead could have registered flat or low-level growth.

Japan continues to play a positive role by assisting East Asian countries, particularly Thailand, Indonesia, and South Korea, in coping with their financial crises. When the crisis began in Thailand, it was not the United States but Japan that first rang warning bells and joined in the International Monetary Fund's (IMF) package of US$17.2 billion to defend the Thai baht. Japan pledged US$4 billion of this total, the same amount offered by the IMF, and China pledged US$1 billion in its first, and so far only, instance of offering funds to stem the crisis. The United States failed to participate.

Japan pledged US$5 billion to the US$40 billion IMF support package to Indonesia, whereas the United States pledged US$3 billion. Japan also offered US$10 billion to the IMF support package of US$57 billion for South Korea, to which the United States contributed US$5 billion. China did not participate in either the Indonesian or the South Korean rescue scheme.

Japan's aggregate support within the framework of IMF rescue packages for Thailand, Indonesia, and South Korea amounted to US$19 billion. That was by far the largest amount by an individual nation—more than half the amount of the IMF's own contribution, more than the World Bank's contribution, and more than twice the U.S. contribution of US$8 billion. Japan claims that its effort to assist these three countries will amount to more than US$40 billion, including export credits from the Japan Export-Import Bank, special yen credits, and technical assistance for financial training and fostering so-called support industries.

JAPAN'S STRUGGLE FOR ITS OWN RECOVERY

Japan has not been able to absorb exports from these financially troubled countries because of its own recession. Japan's global exports from January to May 1998 decreased 4.5 percent compared with the same period the previous year, owing to a sharp drop in exports to East Asian countries. But imports for the same period showed an even larger decline, plunging 17 percent, reflecting the sharp business slowdown.

Japan wishes to play a more positive role in supporting the regional economy, and the government unquestionably recognizes the importance of an accelerated economic recovery, but the recession has narrowed the available options. In early 1997, I wrote that "the Japanese are not unhappy about their present lives, but they are uneasy about the future." I would still assert that the Japanese are not unhappy with their present situation, but they have begun actively worrying about the future, particularly job security, pensions, and the banking sector. Uncertainties about the future have prompted Japanese households to tighten spending, with the result that consumption is falling and inventories are swelling. Negative business prospects have discouraged investment, a situation aggravated by the credit squeeze by commercial banks, which are saddled with the bulk of the domestic nonperforming loans.

The current situation represents a dramatic turnabout from a decade ago. During the bubble economy from 1985 to 1991, the value of real estate assets and stock prices increased ¥1,200 trillion (US$8.6 trillion at US$1 = ¥140). When the bubble collapsed, the same amount, ¥1,200 trillion, was lost from 1992 to 1998. The parties that suffered most were the real estate and construction industries and the commercial banks that lent money on the basis of land collateral appraised at its inflated value.

To boost the post-bubble economy, the government has instituted a series of fiscal stimulus packages during the past six years amounting to ¥70 trillion, in the form of public works investment and special tax cuts. The result was gross domestic product real growth rates of 0.4 percent, 0.5 percent, 0.6 percent, 2.8 percent, and 3.2 percent, respectively, from fiscal 1992 to fiscal 1996. Encouraged by the GDP growth recorded in 1995 and 1996, the government launched a fiscal reform program aimed at curtailing the budget deficit from 5.9 percent to 3.0 percent of GDP by the year 2003 and enforced a tight fiscal policy, including raising the consumption tax and abolishing the special income tax reduction, thereby adding ¥9 trillion to the government's coffers. However, this move proved premature, as the government had overestimated the strength of the economic recovery. The Asian financial crisis aggravated the situation, but most damaging were the recent bankruptcies of some of Japan's leading financial institutions, which had the effect of creating doubt about the credibility of Japanese financial institutions in general.

Another factor—banks' capital needs—brought to the fore the fragility of Japan's financial institutions. In the autumn of 1996, then Prime Minister Hashimoto Ryūtarō pledged to effect a Japanese "big bang" of deregulation measures for the banks as part of a larger financial reform package, and the early implementation of the Bank for International Settlements' requirements for banks' capital adequacy ratios was declared in June 1997. With stock and real estate prices plummeting, banks started tightening credit to borrowers, even to those sound borrowers to whom banks otherwise would have eagerly extended credit. Against this background, the issue of reform of financial institutions—more specifically, the question of how to deal with nonperforming loans—started to become a focus of economic recovery efforts.

The Japanese government has launched three sets of policy measures to reactivate the economy. The first included fiscal stimulus measures amounting to ¥3 trillion implemented in January 1998 and a ¥16 trillion package including a special income tax cut and a large-scale public works program. These measures were expected to inflate the GDP by 2 percent, with the effects becoming evident in the early autumn of 1998. However, these fiscal stimulus measures are just the latest in a series of measures that have totaled ¥70 trillion so far; they will have only a one-time effect.

The second set of measures aims to resolve the problem of nonperforming loans. An outline for these measures was announced in February 1998 bolstered by a fund of ¥30 trillion, of which ¥17 trillion would be used to protect depositors and ¥13 trillion to reinforce capital adequacy. After the House of Councillors election in July 1998, a set of bills for disposing of nonperforming loans and for promoting the liquidation of real estate held as collateral was introduced in the Diet.

The third set focuses on structural reform and deregulation. The government has already made substantial progress in deregulation and now has an organizational structure in place to further advance its efforts. The structural reform efforts center on tax reductions. The government proposes reducing the tax rate for the highest income levels from the current 65 percent to 50 percent and lowering the burden of corporate income taxes from 46.3 percent to 40 percent. Policy debate continues on the best means of compensating for the loss of tax revenue; the probable course will be for the government to both expand the tax base and issue deficit bonds.

Some analysts have voiced suspicions that the Japanese government wants the yen to depreciate further to boost exports and thus spur the economic recovery, but nothing could be further from the truth. Although depreciation of the yen might not hurt Japanese exports, it would seriously damage overall confidence in the economy. When the yen depreciates, stock prices fall. Furthermore, yen depreciation would have the effect of increasing the yen value of overseas assets, thus negatively affecting the banks' ability to satisfy capital adequacy requirements.

Although it is curious that the yen should depreciate vis-à-vis the U.S. dollar despite the substantial—and expanding—current account surplus in Japan's balance of payments, one can argue that as long as there is a sizable difference in interest rates between Tokyo and New York, pressure for yen depreciation will remain.

The question of currency intervention has presumably been a subject of policy debate between Tokyo and Washington. Although little has been revealed about the nature of the debate between the two monetary authorities, one wonders why Washington has been and still is so reluctant to intervene jointly with Japan in the foreign exchange market. Unilateral intervention by Japanese authorities is ineffective, as was clear in mid-April 1998 when the Bank of Japan was reported to have intervened unsuccessfully on a massive scale.

The logic underlying the U.S. reluctance appears to rest on three assumptions:

- It is in the U.S. interest to have a strong dollar vis-à-vis the yen and other currencies. The weaker the yen, the better for the U.S. economy.
- Intervention does not work because the market determines exchange rates.
- It is desirable to force Japan to reform, even if this entails the use of market forces and the expression of dissatisfaction or skepticism.

U.S. Treasury Secretary Rubin, testifying before a Senate subcommittee on June 11, 1998, expressed strong skepticism about the effectiveness of U.S. currency intervention to support the yen. The following day, June 12, Japan's Economic Planning Agency announced that the growth rate for the first quarter was minus 1.2 percent, thus bringing the growth rate for fiscal 1997 to minus 0.7 percent, the first negative growth rate for the Japanese economy in 24 years. The yen tumbled more than ¥6 to ¥145 = US$1 after the announcement, and the Tokyo stock market plunged. But one wonders what motivated Rubin to offer such testimony on the eve of Japan's announcement of poorer-than-expected economic results, which prompted international speculators to sell the yen.

Having followed attentively the deterioration of the Japanese economy for the past few years, I have been struck by the overwhelming role played by psychological factors and declining confidence in Japan's economic performance. In that psychological game, the role played by the U.S. Treasury has been of increasing significance. Wall Street is attentive to and respects the Treasury's views, which are fully reported in the U.S. media. One wonders if the Treasury is fully cognizant of its awesome power and responsibility.

POSTSCRIPT

One year later, the three popular national images of China as the good guy, Japan as the bad guy, and the United States as the prosperous judge have undergone various changes. Japan is still struggling but seems to be over the worst of the recession thanks to concerted efforts by the newly formed Obuchi cabinet, and the prosperity of the United States appears stable. The most dramatic change can be seen in China and China-U.S. relations. There are signs that China will be confronted with many difficult economic problems that might lead to serious internal policy disputes. Most striking is the change in mutual perceptions between China and the United States. The failure of Zhu Rongji during his trips to the United States to conclude negotiations on China's entry to the World Trade Organization, the accidental bombing of the Chinese Embassy in Belgrade in May 1999 by a U.S. B2 bomber, and the January 1999 report by a U.S. House of Representatives Select Committee of Chinese spy activities at U.S. nuclear weapons research institutes—all these have altered what was once heralded as a constructive strategic partnership.

If some Japanese were concerned a year ago that China-U.S. relations were improving at the expense of Japan-U.S. relations, those same Japanese are now concerned that China-U.S. relations will deteriorate to the point of negatively affecting Japan-U.S. relations. Both scenarios point to the intrinsic importance of redoubled efforts to maintain and promote communication and dialogue among the three major powers in Asia Pacific.

CHAPTER V

Beyond the Asian Financial Crisis

Daniel H. Rosen

THE ASIAN FINANCIAL CRISIS of 1997 has affected China, Japan, and the United States not just economically but also in the political and security realms. In terms of three-way China-Japan-U.S. economic relations, in particular, the effects are best discerned by examining two phenomena that predate the crisis. The first is the continuation of economic transition in China. The second is paralysis in Japanese economic policy making.

REVIEW OF THE ASIAN FINANCIAL CRISIS*

The crisis economies have all displayed some combination of a dearth of prudent regulation, a lack of competition, and widespread cronyism. Overvalued currencies with fixed exchange rate regimes undermined stability in this environment. High returns from investments in these economies, partly owing to the artificial strength of the currencies,

---

* As a prefatory note, I plead guilty to attempting to compartmentalize phenomena that in reality are intertwined. Japan's stagnation was both a contributor to and—to the extent that it will be prolonged—a consequence of the larger financial crisis. China's transition has similarly reflected Japanese macroeconomic realities and the fallout from the crisis. In all cases, the actions of other economies in the region have been critically important to shaping constraints and priorities, for the United States as well as for China and Japan. Nonetheless, my concern here is the trilateral relationship.

led to a focus on short-term capital inflows at the expense of less vola-
tile long-term investments. Fragile financial sectors could neither
cope effectively with large inflows of short-term capital nor curb increasing maturity mismatches. In addition, much of the corporate
borrowing for investments in these countries was not hedged against
foreign exchange risk. Signs of market volatility in the region thus
hastened traders' decisions to sell holdings of vulnerable currencies.

Nonproductive investment aggravated financial fragility. Property
sector investment, especially, led to inflated asset bases and property
speculation. The inclination to ignore such realities intensified at the
first sign of trouble. The unwillingness of leaders in several countries
to address the consequences of their policies by making macroeconomic adjustments, cleaning up widespread corruption, or allowing
currencies to adjust naturally and gradually ahead of speculative bet-
ting fueled confidence problems.

Such conditions created the potential for contagion. Because many
developing nations export similar products, one devaluation led to
another, as markets bet that neighbors would have no choice but to
follow suit. Because many countries in the region had similar finan-
cial-sector problems, the logic of attacking one country's currency
was easily extended to others. Rosy assumptions that had benefited
more advanced economies in the region quickly withered.

None of this should have been a surprise. Before Thailand's market collapsed, economic observers ranging from the conservative (the
International Monetary Fund [IMF]) to the maverick (Paul Krug-
man) to the populist (William Greider) had commented on every
aspect of Asia's weakness. Rather, what was surprising is that the two
countries most capable of responding forcefully to the crisis—Japan
and the United States—did not, whereas the one that could have been
forgiven for fumbling—China—exceeded expectations.

China's Transition

China's transition to a market economy has been well documented,
but the depictions of booming construction and consumption in
China's cities have obscured the distance that remains. The biggest
challenge for the trilateral relationship is keeping China on track

toward economic liberalization. The worst-case scenarios for China's economic, political, and security well-being derive from a failure to accomplish that. Clearly, the crisis has made this task harder in the short term by diminishing marginal market growth for Chinese exports and indirectly contributing to a decline in foreign direct investment. In the medium term, we may find that the crisis accelerated certain virtuous domestic reforms, but for now the challenges are greater. In fact, the surprisingly bold World Trade Organization (WTO) accession terms proposed by Zhu Rongji in Washington, D.C., in April 1999 were early evidence that the crisis has accelerated reforms in China.

Although the burden is mostly China's, of course, no one can deny any longer that the actions of Japan and the United States have an important impact on China's position, given the degree to which China is already integrated with the external economy. Therefore, it is appropriate to talk about China's transition in the context of the trilateral relationship, even though managing the transition is China's sovereign affair in narrow terms.

The biggest hurdles in China's transition are as follows:

- Closure, recapitalization, privatization, or reorganization of the remaining state-owned enterprises (SOEs). Although precise figures are hard to confirm, tens of thousands of enterprises, employing over 110 million Chinese as of 1996, remain in state hands. Fewer than 1 percent of these account for more than 50 percent of all recorded SOE profits. If this sector does not become more competitive, 100 million Chinese stand to become unemployed. That is plainly unacceptable to China's leaders. Therefore, if these firms are not made more competitive, the sectors in which they operate cannot be liberalized fully, which puts Chinese economic officials in conflict with Japanese and U.S. officials.
- Weakness in the financial sector. China's financial sector is still programmed to sustain bad investments that should not have been made because they squander scarce resources that should be invested elsewhere. On the consumer side, companies are deprived of adequate financial services to compete well, and households have little opportunity to select worthy savings vehicles and develop sound investment habits.

These aspects of reform would have been the key challenge of the 1990s even without the regional financial meltdown. Postcrisis, the tasks are harder still because volatility has scared away some investors and trade surpluses are trending downward at the same time social costs are rising. However, the Chinese leaders appear to understand the situation.

China can solve its problems by adopting several government policies, with support from Japan and the United States:

- Building the central regulatory capacity needed to allow efficient producers and vendors of goods or services—whether local or foreign—to enter and exit markets and thus compete. This capacity must be designed to protect consumer welfare and be enforceable at the local level.
- Provision of new financial regulations, incentives, and institutions to permit efficient long-term capital intermediation. This will permit better investment in productive economic activity as well as better management of individual wealth, all of which would diversify risk and thus dampen volatility.
- Centrally led investment in professional education, especially at the postsecondary level, to provide for the needs of a complex society, instead of relying on either foreign experts, foreign-educated Chinese, or substandard employees—the three choices employers now face for many critical positions.
- Sustained use of foreign competition to introduce new ideas and technologies, to prod domestic firms to increase productivity and adopt a customer orientation, to lessen parochial Chinese nationalism, and to diversify the risk of local downturns by deepening the globalization of the Chinese economy.

The public and private sectors of Japan and the United States have the ability to support or to hamper these tasks. Expatriates in China too often argue for collusion, exceptional treatment, and devolution of authority away from Beijing. Policymakers and businesspeople alike, on the other hand, ought to ask how they could better support the efforts of Chinese authorities as proposed above.

JAPAN'S PARALYSIS

The biggest surprise from the Asian financial crisis was the weakness of Japan's economic and political institutions. The crisis turned a suspicion into a conclusion: Japan has not yet fully grasped either the nature of its own low domestic growth or its responsibilities in assuming external economic leadership. It should not have been a surprise, however, as Japan's economy has underperformed expectations since 1992.

My colleague Adam Posen of the Institute for International Economics has identified four competing views concerning Japan's stagnation:

- Japan needs deep structural reforms steered by the government before growth can be restored.
- Japan's problems are no longer solvable by vested interests, and a crisis sufficient to destroy old ways is needed to restore growth.
- Japan's current growth slowdown is the inevitable product of demographics, and slogging through is the responsible thing to do for long-term optimality.
- Japan has lost the 1990s as a result of misguided macroeconomic policies.*

Posen accepts a role for factors other than macroeconomic policy, while placing priority on fiscal stimulus and competition. But regardless of which explanation best explains Japan's poor growth, the Japanese authorities have failed to consider the implications of their malaise for neighboring economies looking to their stronger former model for support. Stagnant domestic consumption has dragged down regional market growth, and Japanese producers have crowded other regional developed markets with goods that could not find demand at home. Direct and indirect effects on exchange rates, lending, and direct investment all result from this poor performance to some degree.

One effect on the United States has been a rising trade deficit with Japan. The deficit was exacerbated by a weakening yen as markets lost faith that Japan could restore economic strength through domestic demand growth. This, in turn, has made it difficult politically for the United States to take a leadership stance on economic issues in Asia, including funding the IMF. China has lost export opportunities to serve Japanese consumers but also, and even more important, has lost exchange rate competitiveness from being the only major country not to devalue to match the yen.

* Posen, Adam S. 1998. *Restoring Japan's Economic Growth*. Washington, D.C.: Institute for International Economies.

Japan did not cause the Asian financial crisis of 1997. However, its dithering has undermined regional economic confidence severely since the crisis began and thereby caused unnecessary pain for other Asian economies, many of which, ironically, have emulated Japan until recently.

CONCLUSION

What are the implications of the Asian financial crisis for the trilateral relationship? First, the urgency of the crisis forced all three countries to demonstrate their capacity for leadership and to clarify the thinking of their senior leaders.

- China, by its decision not to devalue the renminbi, encouraged some calm in the region. It was not, in fact, its decision to refrain initially but its subsequent stalwartness that was useful. Although it may be true that China's overall well-being is actually served by not devaluing, given that counter-devaluations would surely follow and the high volume of dollar-denominated re-export content of its exports, there were many domestic interests that preferred a cheaper renminbi. China stood firm because, probably for the first time in its history, its calculus of national welfare took into account the regional and global, not just domestic, economies.

- Japan, meanwhile, unmasked its domestic uncertainty and inflexibility and a preoccupation with domestic vested interests at the expense of regional imperatives. Like the United States, Japan's politics at home ran counter to globalization.

- The United States failed to act decisively at the start of the crisis, choosing not to contribute to the rescue of Thailand and thereby marginally eroding confidence that a broader crisis could be stemmed. In the months that followed, U.S. domestic politics stood in the way of provisioning multilateral financial authorities with the resources they might need to fight further meltdowns, not just in Asia but in Latin America and Europe as well. This is not the strong United States that took decisive steps to head off a financial crisis in Mexico in 1995, but then this is the United States whose president was rebuked severely at home for his willingness to act at that time.

These new parameters for what each of the partners can contribute to international economic leadership suggest new alignments in managing the system. China is willing to contribute more than previously expected and Japan less, at a time when the United States increasingly needs to leverage its own efforts. Thus, the first implication of the crisis is for greater China-U.S. cooperation on economic matters in the future and less emphasis on the Japan-U.S. consensus. This is the net implication of the financial crisis; perhaps facts in other areas will offset these trends at the economic margin. Such a realignment would create anxieties among the three partners and in many other countries as well, but, because it is inevitable, the three countries should make the best effort possible to accomplish it smoothly and without rancor—as difficult as that seems in light of the China-U.S. frictions stemming from the accidental bombing of the Chinese Embassy in Belgrade by the North Atlantic Treaty Organization and allegations of extensive espionage by Chinese agents in the United States.

Second, the crisis has forced us to review our current international economic system. It has raised questions, in particular, concerning the role of macroeconomic monitoring and the availability and use of official funds in the event of emergencies. These are complex questions not easily answered in an overview; designing a new architecture would require Chinese, Japanese, and U.S. participation. Japan and the United States are prone to be distracted from this task by domestic issues and residual bilateral matters, and although China is not likewise distracted to the same extent, it remains outside important forums. For the three-way relationship to be used to maximum benefit, it is imperative that China participate actively in the forums where the system is conceived and managed. Of import here are of course the WTO and the G-8.

Finally, the crisis was, in some ways, a bearer of a type of "creative destruction" that was ripe to occur. The crisis destroyed models of unguarded intervention in commerce by authorities not held to a popular test, inefficient loan portfolios, and projects that foolishly had been allocated scarce resources. It has also laid waste to commonly held beliefs in a commercial alternative to contestable markets and the rule of law. The implication of this is increased long-term potential for healthy economic development along sustainable lines, if social stability can be maintained in the coming, transitional years. For the China-Japan-U.S. economic relationship, that means a chance for invigorated cooperation based on a single set of assumptions, and it means a set of common social objectives instead of the bickering of recent years.

Taking advantage of this chance means working toward economic stability and dynamic change at the same time, in a manner that will necessarily redistribute power and wealth. This redistribution will take place within each of the three partner economies, and among them, and the outcomes may not be equal. By transferring resources to those better able to produce efficiently and competitively, all three nations will generate not only new wealth but also more stable economic underpinnings. But for now, this driving force is less stable than it is dynamic. It portends major adjustments in political alignments, balance of payments surpluses and deficits, and other elements of national accounts—including long-term Chinese debt.

What is required more than anything else during such a process is mutual trust and respect. The China-U.S. summit in Beijing generated a new wealth of trust largely because both sides abandoned long-held formulas for dealing with one another and embraced practical new ones. Sadly, much of that trust has been squandered now over spies, bombs, and the WTO. Let us hope it is not too late to recoup that trust.

CHAPTER VI

Where Does Japan Fit in the China-Japan-U.S. Relationship?

Funabashi Yōichi

PRESIDENT BILL CLINTON'S TRIP to China was a welcome step toward better China-U.S. relations, and the Japanese believe that an enhanced relationship between China and the United States is in their long-term interests both in terms of Japan's own national interest and Japan's relationships with both countries. To see China and the United States de-targeting each other and normalizing relations is, without a doubt, beneficial to the region, particularly to Japan and South Korea.

However, Japanese policymakers feel uneasy about the strategic partnership that has taken shape between China and the United States. The Japanese perceive the partnership as an effort to adulterate the Japan-U.S. alliance. Having made strenuous efforts to enhance security ties with the United States, some Japanese feel used and abused by the Americans. They fear that the United States enhanced its security ties with Japan in 1996 so as to deal with China from a position of strength, whereas Japan does not enjoy similar leverage. Hence, President Clinton's visit further sensitized the emerging perception, particularly in the early months of 1998, that progress in the China-U.S. relationship is being made at Japan's expense.

Neither Japan nor the United States has dealt effectively with this perception.

Secretary of State Madeleine Albright visited Prime Minister Hashimoto Ryūtarō to brief him on the presidential trip to China, but he was neither impressed nor convinced by her overtures. Hashimoto did not get a feel for the strategic drive and long-term purpose of President Clinton's visit to China. He was not alone in feeling that way. This uncertainty poses a big stumbling block for Japan; Japan must always guess as to the nature of the United States' long-term strategy in Asia and where the Japan-U.S. alliance and the new China policy fit in the overall picture.

In contrast to the early 1970s, when Prime Minister Satō Eisaku was blamed for being belittled by the Americans and allowing the United States to strike a deal with China over Japan's head, we have not witnessed the emergence of an anti-incumbent power struggle in Japan. However, there is a general uneasiness and a shared dissatisfaction toward the United States. Some Japanese political leaders feel that their loyalty to the Japan-U.S. security alliance has been grossly compromised. Such loyalty is regarded as one of the highest virtues in Japan's value system and, given the backdrop of Japan's worst economic depression since World War II, many Japanese feel that the United States is further damaging Japanese feelings that have been hurt already.

Nevertheless, future Japan-U.S. relations cannot be predicted based on current factors. Many Japanese feel that owing to differing political systems and lifestyles, China and the United States are a long way from solidifying their relationship. On the other hand, the Japanese will probably remember the Clinton administration's indifference to Japan at this critical moment for some time.

New Perceptions
about the Trilateral Relationship

Some observers perceive a China-U.S. bipolarity, or virtual bipolarity, developing. Others believe that the United States is pursuing ties with China at the expense of the Japan-U.S. relationship. Furthermore, many contend that China is a nation on the rise, whereas Japan is a nation in decline. The United States is keenly aware of Japanese wariness as a result of these perceptions, and so we have heard for some time assurances that the China-Japan-U.S. relationship should not develop at the expense of the Japan-U.S. relationship. However, these assurances have not fully appeased the Japanese.

Even though the "strategic partnership" between China and the United States may be merely a public relations ploy, it is nevertheless problematic. The partnership may tempt Japan and other Asian nations to seek similar treatment from China.

The perception that China is on the rise and Japan on the decline could also intensify Japan's sense of rivalry with China. In Tokyo, China's pressure on Japan and the United States to intervene to stop the yen's further depreciation seemed somewhat self-serving: Intervention would give the Chinese a good excuse to devalue the renminbi. Therefore, Japan feels as if it has become a scapegoat.

Perhaps China suspects that the United States and Japan conspired to allow the yen to depreciate so as to boost Japanese exports while denying China the same opportunity. On the other hand, Japan feels that China and the United States colluded to bring up the "Japan problem" so as to avert an Asian backlash against the U.S. "victory" in the Asian financial markets and China's rise as an economic center.

Challenges to Managing the Trilateral Relationship

There appears to be ambiguity in the U.S. position with regard to the "markets vs. politics" and the "liberalization vs. stability" debates. For example, the United States apparently wishes to keep Chinese financial markets highly regulated and maintain the value of the renminbi. Some Japanese politicians feel that the United States applies a double standard to China as opposed to the rest of Asia, praising China for regulating while condemning other countries for doing the same.

Given the recent turmoil in Asian markets, there is little incentive for the Chinese monetary authorities to pursue liberalization or to discuss macroeconomic policy. At the same time, the United States wants to maintain the status quo in Chinese financial markets. Thus, it is difficult for China, Japan, and the United States to consult on macroeconomic policies, let alone coordinate them.

South Asian nuclear issues could yet cause some friction as we are seeing the emergence of a dividing line between the nuclear haves and the have-nots. Recently, China acted to exclude Japan's participation in the Geneva conference of the established nuclear powers. Historical and psychological tensions remain between Japan and the United States, as shown by the Smithsonian Hiroshima Panel disputes in 1995. Japan's aspirations to vocally endorse nuclear disarmament have effectively been compromised, and the nation feels that it is being "contained." Some even feel that the United States and China are ganging up on Japan.

Japan has explored various new strategic dimensions. First was the global partnership between the George Bush administration and the Kaifu Toshiki cabinet that collapsed after Japan's inability to cope with the Gulf crisis. Then came the new Asianist school, which failed because Japan could not envisage cooperation between China and Japan as a leadership core in the region. The obstacles to Sino-Japanese cooperation were history and Taiwan. Finally, the Indonesian meltdown undermined any ideas of an Asian solution to regional security. An Asia-Pacific Economic Cooperation driven regional strategy also stalled when Japan and the rest of Asia were hit hard in the Asian economic crisis.

JAPANESE DOMESTIC POLITICS

There is a trend toward inward-looking politics and especially anti-American, anti-Treasury sentiments in Japan. A new sense of rivalry with China is emerging, but, oddly enough, there is also keener interest in strengthening relations with China. Many analysts feel that at the root of the United States' "Japan passing" phenomenon is the lack of a deeper understanding and cooperation between China and Japan.

As it searches for new economic reference points, Japan is showing its uneasiness with U.S. economic models through renewed interest in European systems and reforms. On the political front, the government is interested in normalizing relations with Russia, but this does not hold much appeal for the general public. Indeed, Japan lags behind other nations in normalizing relations with Russia.

The Liberal Democratic Party is much discredited for its gross mismanagement of the economy, which has resulted in an excessive focus on the domestic economy and little attention being paid to foreign policy initiatives. In the meantime, various reform agendas are now in limbo owing to the urgency of stimulating the dampened economy. In a macro-economic sense, Japan still seems stagnated. However, on the micro level Japan is witnessing the emergence of new players, new rules, new energies, new spirit, and new dynamics. It remains to be seen how they will shape domestic politics.

Looking back over the 1990s, the burden of history seems to have been as equally an important factor as the economy in Japan's woes. Japan's problems started the day the cold war ended. Japan has had difficulty adjusting to the new environment—in particular, the Clinton administration's new foreign policy priorities and the rise of China—and in a way is paying a high price for the inertia of its political system, once a success story of the cold war.

CHAPTER VII

Causes and Implications of the South Asian Nuclear Tests

Ni Feng

SUBSEQUENT TO INDIA'S FIVE NUCLEAR TESTS on May 11 and 13, 1998, Pakistan conducted six tests of its own on May 28 and 30, exacerbating tensions between the two South Asian countries. As India's stance on developing nuclear weapons showed no sign of softening, Pakistan indicated that it could not unilaterally withdraw from the nuclear race. The two countries will now likely focus on developing the necessary delivery and support systems.

This new nuclear arms race in South Asia may be the most important global issue at the century's end. It threatens not only peace and stability in South Asia but also international security.

MOTIVATIONS BEHIND THE INDIAN NUCLEAR TESTS

Indian Defense Minister George Fernandes has declared China to be India's "potential number one threat," and in a letter to President Bill Clinton on May 13, Indian Prime Minister Atal Bahari Vajpayee asserted that India's nuclear tests were justified due to a weakening of national security. Vajpayee stated, "We have an overt nuclear weapons state on our borders, a state which committed armed aggression against India in 1962, and an atmosphere of distrust persists mainly due to the unresolved border problem" (Vajpayee 1998). The Indian Bharatiya Janata Party (BJP)–led administration thus posited that its nuclear tests were due to perceived threats from China because of the border dispute and the 1962 war. However, this was not the real reason behind India's recent nuclear tests. We need to consider a number of factors to explain the motivation behind the nuclear tests.

First is India's domestic political needs. In fact, India has had the ability to produce nuclear weapons for several years, and Indian officials have said on several occasions that India has mastered "all nuclear weapon technologies" and that if necessary could "assemble atom bombs immediately." According to estimates, India has the capability to produce about fifty nuclear bombs and plutonium devices.

India's security has recently improved. Notably, new progress has been made in the dialogue between India and Pakistan. For example, in February 1997 Mohd Nawaz Sharif of the Pakistan Muslim League rejected war as an option for resolving disputes between the two countries, saying, "Pakistan and India must solve the Kashmir dispute bilaterally. We must sit at the table, face to face, to study and solve all outstanding disputes" (Xinhua News Agency 1997). India responded to this signal immediately, with then Prime Minister H. D. Deve Gowda expressing his wish to initiate a new dialogue with Pakistan in a letter to Sharif congratulating him on his election as prime minister.

With these overtures marking a turning point in the relationship, talks between top-level leaders of the two countries have been more frequent than ever before. In 1997, there were four rounds of talks between the two prime ministers, three formal sessions at the diplomatic secretarial level, and other talks between the ministers of foreign affairs. Moreover, the two countries could claim some real achievements, including formalizing a list of issues to be resolved, and both sides reached some concrete understandings, such as agreeing to set up specialized working groups. This is in striking contrast to the seven rounds of talks held intermittently between 1989 and 1994, all of which came to a fruitless conclusion. Although many discussions were held in the past between the prime ministers of the two countries, most resulted in little more than an exchange of greetings and avoided contentious issues. But since early 1997, the leaders of both countries have adopted a comparatively realistic attitude. In addition, the two prime ministers now inform each other of urgent problems via a hotline, and they frequently exchange opinions. Some actual problems have thus been resolved. For example, the conflicts that arose over the demarcation of Kashmir in September and early October 1997 were quelled through hotline communications between the two prime ministers.

Sino-Indian relations have also improved in recent years. India is one of China's largest neighbors, and the two countries have traditionally been friends. During the initial post-independence period for both countries, Sino-Indian relations were quite amicable. Indeed, both China and India were early advocates of the Five Principles of Peaceful Coexistence. In the late 1950s, however, relations between the two nations began to deteriorate. A boundary question has been the core issue among the many points of contention between the two countries, causing the Sino-Indian border war in 1962.

Since the mid-1980s, a number of events have augured improvements in Sino-Indian relations, following an exchange of visits between the late Indian Prime Minister Rajiv Gandhi and Chinese Premier Li Peng. In September 1993, then Indian Prime Minister P. V. Narasimha Rao visited China, and China and India signed an agreement to maintain peace and tranquillity along demarcation lines in their border areas. Indian defense experts came to recognize that détente with China would be to India's benefit, by creating a stable environment, reducing the defense budget, and helping to develop the economy. Abid Hussain, deputy director of the Indian Institute for Contemporary Studies, wrote in *Pioneer* in November 1993 that India should devote itself to developing its economy, striving to become a major global economic power within twenty-five years, and thus bringing about a peaceful and stable environment (Yu 1998, 3).

In November 1996, Chinese President Jiang Zemin paid a state visit to India. At the conclusion of cordial discussions, the top leaders of the two countries signed four agreements, including a pact covering confidence-building measures for military forces along demarcation lines in border areas. During President Jiang's visit, Indian Prime

Minister Gowda disregarded diplomatic protocol and appeared at the airport in person to receive and to see off the Chinese leader. This showed India's readiness to elevate Sino-Indian relations to a new, higher level. After the visit, China and India made some progress in such areas as recognizing present border demarcations, reducing bilateral military forces in border areas, establishing confidence-building measures, and opening border areas to free trade. In early 1998, Chinese Defense Minister Chi Haotian visited India.

These examples suggest that the Indian security environment has shown some improvement. So why did the Indian government conduct nuclear tests at this time? It is instructive to observe the current Indian domestic political situation. After Prime Minister Inder Kumar Gujral fell from power in November 1997, Indian politics entered a turbulent period. The BJP took over the government as the dominant member of a coalition early in 1998, but the political basis of the coalition is weak, with the coalition government claiming a single-seat majority in the Indian Congress. Also significant in the Indian political climate is the fact that the policy of developing nuclear weapons has had broad popular support for a long time. In 1997, for example, several public opinion polls indicated that 60 percent of the Indian people supported nuclear weapons development. As a result, the BJP regarded nuclear tests as a strategic move, rather like a chess gambit, that would further the party's interests and improve the political situation. The party's main objectives were to stimulate nationalistic emotions among Indians by creating a controversy of global proportions, to divert the attention of the Indian people and the media from domestic issues, and to strengthen its position as the party in power.

The party also regarded the tests as a form of strategic deterrent, mainly aimed at China and Pakistan. In the post–cold war period, nuclear weapons are almost impossible to use as a tool in actual combat, but they still play a deterrent role. Some political and military figures in India regard China as a potential threat and entertain grave concerns about China's power. Specifically, they claim that China's nuclear power poses a serious threat to India's security and that sales of Chinese weapons to Pakistan would disturb the existing military balance between India and Pakistan. For this reason, India is making great efforts to develop its nuclear and missile technologies, and it refuses to waive its nuclear option. By carrying out nuclear tests, India displayed its nuclear capabilities to China, Pakistan, and other South Asian countries, and it engaged in strategic deterrence.

India also regards nuclear tests as a means of seeking major power status. India's international status has weakened in recent years. The collapse of the cold war order in the early 1990s sent shock waves throughout South Asia. The U.S.-Pakistan axis ceased to exist, and the Soviet-Indian alliance fell apart. The end of the cold war also rendered the nonaligned movement meaningless, and India's leadership in that movement fell victim to the ongoing drastic change. On the other hand, China, Japan, and the Association of Southeast Asian Nations (ASEAN) have seen their status elevated vis-à-vis that of India among Asian entities as a result of their bolstered economic and political prowess. Given India's aspirations to major power status, the actual situation conflicts with Indian government objectives.

In addition, India wants to join the Asia-Pacific Economic Cooperation (APEC) forum. APEC recently admitted three new member states, but not India. APEC has since vowed not to accept any new members, implying that nonmember India will continue to suffer from a serious handicap in foreign trade.

The Indian government desires to be a powerful and respected member of the international community and views permanent membership in the UN Security Council as a way to raise its status. However, its competitors in this race—Japan and Germany—are more likely to gain permanent membership.

Among the Indian Ocean Rim nations, India, Australia, and South Africa are the leaders, but this nascent partnership cannot compare with the influence of APEC, the European Union (EU), ASEAN, or the North American Free Trade Agreement (NAFTA) area. Any affiliation among Indian Ocean nations does not yet have any permanent significance, and it is premature to forecast whether this region will foster greater economic cooperation in the future.

India is a regional power on the South Asian subcontinent, but its international status faces great challenges. It is clear that the Indian government wants to use its status as a nuclear power to raise its international standing and to enable it to become a permanent UN Security Council member.

Pakistan's Reaction to the Indian Tests

India has long regarded Pakistan as its greatest single threat, and vice versa. This mutual hostility means that both countries regard the development of nuclear weapons as an important means by which to intimidate the other country. Pakistan, which is inferior to India in national strength and conventional weapons, believes that developing nuclear capabilities is the most economical way of challenging India. In Pakistan, the development of nuclear weapons is the only issue on which the whole country is united. Like India, Pakistan has not signed the Nonproliferation Treaty (NPT) to prohibit nuclear tests. Pakistan declares that only if India gives up its nuclear program can Pakistan consider suspending its own. In 1997, Prime Minister Sharif said, "I believe in a world without nuclear weapons. Once India signs the nuclear non-proliferation treaty, Pakistan will follow suit. India has carried out nuclear tests, and it refuses to sign the nuclear non-proliferation treaty. Under these circumstances, it is absolutely unfair to expect Pakistan to halt its nuclear program, which is completely defensive in nature" (Wu 1998, 4). Hence, it is difficult to break the nuclear deadlock between the two countries. After India carried out nuclear tests, Pakistan's national security faced enormous pressure from India. Later, even though relations between China and Pakistan as a whole have been quite amicable, the Chinese government expressed "deep regret" over Pakistan's announcement that it had exploded six nuclear devices.

Fallout from the Nuclear Tests

The nuclear tests constituted a severe blow to international efforts to prevent nuclear weapons proliferation. Remarkable achievements have been made in international arms control and disarmament since the end of the cold war. In particular, a consensus has been reached on preventing proliferation of weapons of mass destruction. The nuclear explosions in South Asia, however, have defeated these sustained efforts by the international community. As UN Secretary-General Kofi Annan pointed out, India's nuclear tests have violated the common understanding reached by the international community.

It is no longer difficult for a country to obtain nuclear technology, due to increasing levels of technological development and exchanges. The key factors today, however, are a commitment not to develop nuclear weapons and a guarantee that the technology will be used for peaceful purposes. A few nations are undoubtedly still seeking to develop nuclear weapons, but their failure to do so to date can be mainly attributed to international pressure. The Indian and Pakistani tests may now touch off a chain reaction, giving other nations an excuse to develop nuclear weapons in the name of national security. If so, the existing international nonproliferation system, which suffers from various shortcomings and fails to achieve sufficient strength in deterrence, will exist in name only.

In addition, the South Asian nuclear tests may have a negative effect on other areas of international arms control and disarmament. Some existing nuclear powers, for example, might now be more reluctant to reduce their nuclear weapons stockpiles. The U.S. Congress could use the tests as justification for postponing ratification of the Comprehensive Test Ban Treaty (CTBT), and the Russian Duma could suspend ratification of the treaty on second-phase strategic arms reduction. These two countries might also reevaluate the negative implications of their nuclear disarmament efforts and thereby reject further cuts.

The recent tests can be regarded as a challenge to the new concept of global security. As the danger of a world war receded with the collapse of the former Soviet Union, peace and development became global themes. Most countries have surrendered traditional security paradigms centering on military force and have formulated new long-term national security strategies stressing technological and economic development.

These states have recognized that mutual reliance rather than mutual destruction is key to their national security. In line with this new security conception, many countries, including India and Pakistan, have used official and unofficial channels to seek cooperation from others on security issues in recent years. However, the recent nuclear tests have ended cooperation on security issues in South Asia and challenged the validity of the newly formed security paradigms themselves.

India's tests also reminded the international community that when a country fails to resolve its internal problems and to develop economically, and when it tries to enhance its overall national capabilities and raise its international status, it may choose nonconventional weapons as the means to do so. It is a matter of concern that some countries may seriously consider developing weapons of mass destruction to maintain security and pursue foreign policy goals. Such thinking is dangerous to the maintenance of global security.

Avoiding Further Nuclear Proliferation

The first step to take in response to the South Asian nuclear tests is to enhance international cooperation on nuclear nonproliferation, especially among the major powers. The international community has already taken some positive steps in response to the crisis. For example, the foreign ministers of the five permanent members (P-5) of the UN Security Council met in Geneva on June 4, 1998, to discuss the nuclear tests in South Asia. The purpose of the P-5 meeting was to coordinate joint efforts to halt the nuclear arms race in South Asia and to restore peace and stability in this region.

The G-8 major industrial powers had the opportunity at their annual summit meeting, held in the spring of 1998 in Birmingham, England, to take an initial collective stance that would respond firmly and unambiguously to India's actions. The group issued a final communiqué calling for stricter export controls on weapons of mass destruction and their delivery systems. The G-8 leaders also pledged to boost the exchange of information on the arms trade.

The G-8 foreign ministers held another meeting in London on June 12, 1998. As part of an effort to increase the number of participants, several other countries, including Argentina, Brazil, South Africa, and the Philippines, were also invited to the meeting. The major powers thus aimed to broaden international support for the process that began with the meeting of the P-5 in Geneva. On nuclear nonproliferation and disarmament, the G-8 has asked India and Pakistan to sign the Fissile Material Cut-off Treaty, the CTBT, and the NPT; to reduce mutual tensions and adopt confidence-building measures; to abandon their nuclear weapons and plans to build nuclear arsenals; and to enter a dialogue on divisive issues.

During President Bill Clinton's visit to China in June 1998, the China-U.S. statement issued by Presidents Jiang and Clinton referred to the South Asian nuclear tests, and both countries condemned the tests by India and Pakistan.

These efforts have produced good results, but they are not enough. The international community should be better coordinated, with the emphasis on persuading India and Pakistan to sign the CTBT. The global community should also work to reduce tensions between India and Pakistan. Given that the hostile relations between India and Pakistan led to both countries conducting nuclear tests, the international community should encourage India and Pakistan to continue their dialogue on security issues.

Whether India and Pakistan enter into a dialogue and their relations show substantive improvement primarily depends on whether there are any breakthroughs in the stalemate over Kashmir. Two wars have failed to settle the issue decisively, and in any case it would be impossible for the winner to annex the territory claimed by the loser. Today, with both countries possessing nuclear capabilities, any conflict between them might turn into a nuclear war. Fortunately, discussions between the two countries last year suggested that there was little possibility of either side choosing the war option. The leaders of both countries have seemingly reached an understanding that totally hostile relations will exact a high price from both parties. The wisest choice is to alleviate this tense situation by continuing to put relations between the two countries on a more positive standing, as was achieved last year, to reach a breakthrough and finally resolve the Kashmir dispute through peaceful negotiations. Such a choice satisfies the interests of both countries and conforms to the current worldwide trend toward peaceful conflict resolution.

India's and Pakistan's nuclear tests and race to develop a carrier rocket have threatened peace and stability in Asia Pacific. As big powers enjoying influence within the region, China, Japan, and the United States can and should act positively to prevent the situation from deteriorating. China is contiguous to India and Pakistan, China-Pakistani relations are good, and Sino-Indian relations have improved gradually since the mid-1980s. During the cold war, the United States and Pakistan were allies, and relations with India are an important component of current U.S. South Asia policy. Japan is a principal source of economic aid to India and Pakistan. More important is that the three countries' stances on the nuclear tests are the same. During President Clinton's visit to Beijing in June 1998, China and the United States issued a joint statement condemning the nuclear tests. Japan not only denounced India's and Pakistan's behavior, but it also is a model of a country that chooses not to exercise its ability to develop nuclear weapons. Persuading India and Pakistan to discontinue their efforts to develop nuclear weapons and carrier rockets and to enter the international nuclear nonproliferation regime as early as possible will both contribute to peace and stability in the region and conform to the three countries' interests. On this issue, China, Japan, and the United States should coordinate their policies so as to expand their cooperative base.

BIBLIOGRAPHY

Vajpayee, Atal Bahari. 1998. Letter to President Clinton, cited in the *New York Times* (13 May).

Wu Xianbing. 1998. "The Motivation of Pakistani Nuclear Tests." Paper presented to the Conference on the Southern Asia Situation after the Nuclear Tests, Institute of Asia-Pacific Studies with the Chinese Academy of Social Sciences, Beijing, China, 6 June.

Xinhua News Agency. 1997. "Pakistan Holds Parliament Election." Dispatch of 4 February.

Yu Hailian. 1998. "The Motivation of Indian Nuclear Tests." Paper presented to the Conference on the Southern Asia Situation after the Nuclear Tests, Institute of Asia-Pacific Studies with the Chinese Academy of Social Sciences, Beijing, China, 6 June.

CHAPTER VIII

Developments on the Korean Peninsula and in Trilateral Relations

Lee Jong Won

THIS CHAPTER EXAMINES changes in South and North Korea in the context of the roles of China-Japan-U.S. trilateral relations in recent developments on the Korean peninsula. The intention is not to disregard or diminish the importance of the internal dynamics in the two Koreas; rather, it is to focus on the consensus about the need for stability on the Korean peninsula. The chapter then looks at the impact of the Korean issue on developments in relations among China, Japan, and the United States.

CHANGES IN THE TWO KOREAS

Exhausted from a decade of nuclear crisis, the two Koreas seemed since 1997 to be looking for a more stable modus vivendi. The Korean Peninsula Energy Development Organization (KEDO) started operating in August 1997 after three years' delay, and the first Four-Party Talks, involving the two Koreas, China, and the United States, were held in Geneva that December.

Inter-Korean governmental contacts initially failed to bear tangible fruit. The second round of Four-Party Talks, held in March 1998, was adjourned when the North remained adamant that the withdrawal of U.S. troops from the peninsula had to be part of the official agenda. A vice-ministerial meeting, conducted in Beijing in April 1998 to discuss trading South Korean fertilizer for concessions from the North on reuniting families separated since the Korean War, did not result in a breakthrough. The overture proved to be premature as Pyongyang was not prepared to accept inflows of people from outside.

The Four-Party Talks had evolved as a compromise. North Korea reluctantly accepted the formula in order to achieve its foremost policy objective of establishing a relationship with the United States. The South had failed to corner the North into accepting an inter-Korean formula and, since it did not want to be alienated from diplomatic initiatives concerning the peninsula, it agreed to the Four-Party scheme as a way of maintaining its influence. Given the South's insistence on and the North's resistance to official inter-Korean talks, the Four-Party recipe was not the first choice of either Korea. But the retreat of Kim Dae Jung's government from previous governments' attempts to prevail on the North by establishing an inter-Korean framework means that the Four-Party Talks may become relatively more important.

The South did not expect immediate results from vice-ministerial contacts, so Pyongyang's quick response to the overtures from President Kim were received with surprise. North Korea may have been testing the will and ability of its new counterpart. Whatever the motivation, that North Korea agreed to have official contact with the South after three years of vehement rejection of the idea was important. Also noteworthy was the fact that the usual exchange of harsh, reproachful words did not accompany the failure of the meeting in Beijing.

Pyongyang had been in a wartime situation of de facto military rule. The Supreme People's Council, the North Korean equivalent of a parliament, was suspended, and the military became even more omnipresent in society. In late 1997, signs of change appeared. The official media declared that the hardest period of the "long march of suffering" had ended, and, in the official and essential step needed to revert from the wartime system to normalcy, an election for the Supreme People's Council Representatives was scheduled for July 1998. The fiftieth anniversary of the Democratic People's Republic of Korea on September 9, 1998, was to be the consummation of this normalizing process.

In tandem with political restructuring, economic cooperation with the South was accelerated. In a symbolic example, Chung Ju Young, president of the Hyundai group, received permission to cross the Demilitarized Zone with trucks of cows as presents to the people of North Korea. During the crisis years, Pyongyang adamantly opposed opening the demarcation line for direct contact between the two Koreas. Maintaining a certain level of tension across the border was an essential part of its brinkmanship. Even humanitarian aid had to be transported by sea, or via China.

The North also announced plans to establish free export zones in Nampo and Wonsan. Different from the secluded Rajin-Sunbong special economic district in the North's far northeast, these two cities are close to the North's political and economic heartland. It is still unclear how far Pyongyang is willing to go in economic opening to the world, but a free export zone in Nampo might be a leap toward Chosun-style market socialism—despite consistent official denials of following a China model.

The policy reversals of the South are an important part of the emerging scene. President Kim's "Sunshine Policy" is based on criticism of previous policies. With the demise of the cold war and the collapse of the Soviet Union, Seoul pursued variations of "unification by absorption." The success of this strategy depended on several conditions. First, the Stalinist state would only be able to survive if ties with its traditional allies—China and the Soviet Union—remained intact. Second, with its vibrant and expanding economy, Seoul would have enough diplomatic influence to isolate Pyongyang. Third, the oppressive and unpopular leadership in the North would disintegrate quickly if external pressure were reinforced. Developments have proven these prerequisites to be nonexistent, if not false.

Ironically, the South Korean quest for the "Koreanization" of the Korean problem resulted instead in its "internationalization." The more Seoul tried to contain Pyongyang within an inter-Korean framework in which it could prevail, the more it lost diplomatic influence. The centers of diplomacy on Korea subsequently became New York, Geneva, and Beijing, where the Four-Party Talks, KEDO, and United Nations–initiated food assistance programs are respectively based.

Learning from earlier failures, Kim Dae Jung tried to regain the diplomatic initiative for the South by building a basis for mutual confidence between the two Koreas. After his inauguration, he officially renounced the policy of "unification by absorption" and suggested that instead of immediate unification, the emphasis would be on peaceful coexistence. This approach, in short, is based on the status quo. Some South Korean nationalists perceive it to be a betrayal of the primary goal of unification, a perpetuation of the division of the fatherland, and as playing into the hands of surrounding powers. However, Kim feels that normalizing South-North relations is the only way to restore "Korea-centeredness" to diplomacy concerning the peninsula. The reasoning is that, once military tension is reduced, Seoul could return to center stage since it is Pyongyang's major source of economic assistance and investment. Such a situation would also be in the long-term interests of Korea's neighbors, given that some form of economic integration with the South is integral to any lasting solution to the North's economic difficulties and to Northeast Asia's stability.

So far, President Kim has successfully rallied majority domestic political support for his Sunshine Policy. No significant organized resistance to his bold initiatives toward rapprochement with the North has yet emerged. The new policies have been welcomed warmly, if not enthusiastically, and his leadership in reversing previous policies—particularly toward the North and Japan—has resulted in high approval ratings for his presidency. This is a remarkable phenomenon, considering conservatives' deep-rooted suspicions about Kim's ideological orientation. A couple of reasons can be identified. The first is generational change. South Koreans born after the Korean War are assuming leading roles in many areas of society and they do not share their parents' antipathy toward the North. In previous administrations, conservative voices were overrepresented in the policy-making process. The second is the ironic impact of the economic crisis. The crisis undercut the South's economic power, the material basis of the hard-line policy. Even conservative nationalists have had to accept the new reality that the South has only limited means to prevail over the North. Soliciting international support for his approach and drawing the North into his new scheme were the next tasks for President Kim.

U.S.-Chinese "Strategic Partnership"

Normalization on the Korean peninsula progressed in tandem with rapprochement between the United States and China after 1996, with Korea becoming a testing ground for the emergent U.S.-China "constructive strategic partnership" in Northeast Asia. The initial record was fairly successful. Even though it is not clear how closely China was involved in the origin of the Four-Party formula, at least in its implementation China's role and contribution have been substantial. In May 14, 1998, testimony to the U.S. House Committee on Foreign Relations, Assistant Secretary of State Stanley Roth raised North Korean policy as a conspicuous example of the U.S.-China strategic dialogue "pay[ing] important results."

For its own reasons, Beijing stepped up political and material support to Pyongyang in recent years, particularly since the death of Kim Il Sung. China provided one million tons of food assistance in 1997, making up for almost half of the North's annual food shortage, and an increasing number of Chinese agricultural and industrial experts are reportedly visiting the North. China's influence over North Korea declined abruptly in the early 1990s when Beijing stopped treating Pyongyang as a special ally and began tilting toward Seoul. Several reasons can be cited for China once again embracing its former ally. First, China's own phenomenal economic growth in the 1990s has enabled it to provide material support. Second, the generational change in the North Korean leadership following the death of Kim Il Sung made it urgent for China to build new relations with the North. Third, China began to perceive the total collapse of North Korea as a real possibility, and it has good reason to fear a power vacuum, massive numbers of refugees fleeing across the border, and other chaotic circumstances.

Together with emerging direct relations with the United States, the North received some "reassurance" from China's reinforced material assistance, and perhaps its siege mentality was lessened somewhat. How China regained "influence" over its troubling socialist neighbor is a process worth examining more closely, as it might provide significant lessons for policy making toward a rogue state.

The U.S.-China "strategic partnership," a transitional substitute for a post–cold war security framework for North Korea, is based on shared interest in maintaining the status quo on the peninsula and in preventing a sudden North Korean collapse.

However, maintaining the status quo is not a static process. Broad reforms are essential for North Korea to survive and remain existent as a society. Such changes—regardless of what they are called—will inevitably have to incorporate market economic characteristics. The fundamental dilemma for Pyongyang will be that Seoul's economic and political gravitational pull may build up inside the secluded regime as economic opening and reforms progress. This dilemma will be unique to North Korea—no such equivalent exists for socialist countries such as China, Vietnam, and Russia.

Present thoughts about scenarios beyond the status quo remain abstract, although such scenarios could obviously influence current policy options. Policy and academic discussions and studies on the postunification security system in Korea stress the desirability of a unified Korea being democratic, peaceful, and nonnuclear. Moderates in both Seoul and Washington emphasize the need to maintain mutual security ties, even after unification. The analogy is made to the choice of postwar Japan to pursue being a "trading state" with minimum military spending. Keeping the United States committed to the Northeast Asian region could spare Korea the political pressure and burden of building up its military to counter its neighbors. However, such expansion of the U.S.-centered alliance system may result in China feeling threatened close to its border.

The "strategic partnership" between the United States and China has been instrumental in stabilizing the Korean peninsula and it will remain important to regional security. If the two powers regress to their confrontation of old, the Korean peninsula will be the first to be critically affected. To ensure the "partnership," it is also necessary to begin talking about postunification Korea.

Japan's Strategic Hesitancy

The passive policy of Japan—the third pillar of the trilateral relationship—toward the Korean peninsula stands in sharp contrast with the more active policies of China and the United States vis-à-vis Korea. Postwar Japan has shied away from articulating a strategy toward

Korea for a few understandable reasons. First, Japan is dependent on the United States to defend its interests in the region. Second, the memory of Japanese colonial domination still makes Koreans wary of any hint of Japanese involvement on the peninsula. Third, prevalent antiwar sentiments in Japan have made discussion of national security a general political taboo. Fourth, imbued with postwar democracy, the Japanese public have resented "colluding" with South Korea's dictatorship.

However, Japan has pursued its strategic interests on the peninsula in its own way. In addition to its indirect contribution to U.S.-Japan security arrangements, Japan did make certain moves of its own when the status quo on the peninsula was seriously challenged. In the early 1970s, Tokyo made strategic approaches to Pyongyang when it was groping for a post–Nixon Doctrine security framework. The formula of cross-recognition of the two Koreas was discussed between the United States, Japan, and possibly China as an integral part of Nixon's grand strategy in the region. When President Carter announced the withdrawal of U.S. troops from Korea, Japan moved actively to reverse the decision. In the early 1980s, when South Korea languished in political and economic turmoil, the Nakasone cabinet made a historic decision to provide US$4 billion of "national security assistance" to the military regime of General Chun Doo Hwan. Kanemaru Shin's mission to Pyongyang in 1990 would be another recent example of a Japanese initiative toward Korea.

Subsequently, Japan has maintained a detached attitude toward North Korea. Tokyo's apparent coolness toward Pyongyang in recent years is conspicuous, considering recent developments on the Korean peninsula. Japan has declined to contribute to UN food assistance programs for the North, even though it has large annual surplus stocks of rice for which it has to pay storage. It objected to the admission of North Korea into the World Bank, the International Monetary Fund, and the Asian Development Bank. When negotiating to normalize relations with North Korea, the Japanese government risked wrecking the whole process by raising the issue of Japanese kidnapped by North Koreans. These negotiations have remained suspended since 1992.

During the nuclear crisis, these attitudes were understood to reflect policy coordination among Seoul, Tokyo, and Washington.

The South Korean government kept a close eye on negotiations between Japan and North Korea. Yet the end of the crisis did not result in a change to the Japanese position. In a halfhearted response to a series of diplomatic offensives by Pyongyang in 1997, Tokyo agreed to resume the long-suspended talks in principle—on the precondition that the kidnapping cases were solved satisfactorily.

Japan's inaction and passivity can be explained in terms of the following. First, in today's Japanese diplomacy the Korean problem is given lower priority than the building of a new balance-of-power formula with regional powers such as China and Russia. Second, domestic opposition to diplomatic recognition of North Korea is still strong among conservatives both in and out of the Liberal Democratic Party. Ad hoc initiatives by politicians such as Kanemaru are severely criticized. Third, the human rights of the kidnapped are very real issues to Japanese, with widespread and deep-rooted public suspicion and rejection of North Korea resulting. The nuclear crisis further blotted Pyongyang's image.

In short, most obstacles to Japanese diplomacy vis-à-vis Korea are domestic in origin. Conversely, the lack of a grand strategy also induces domestic factors to meddle in diplomacy toward Korea. Considering its economic power and its historical ties with the peninsula, Japan's active and constructive role should be encouraged.

The Korean Peninsula and Trilateral Relations

Due to its geographical location, the Korean peninsula is a touchstone of the trilateral relationship among China, Japan, and the United States. Experiences this past century show that rivalry over the peninsula leads to region-wide instability and catastrophic war. A concerted framework involving the countries surrounding Korea is indispensable for the region's stability.

Several points should be stressed in this context. First, if the "concert of powers" results in the institutionalization of classic power politics, then suspicion and resistance from Asian countries—including both Koreas—are inevitable.

Second, in order to have lasting influence trilateral cooperation should be based on shared interests as well as shared values and visions.

Third, trilateral cooperation best serves the region when it functions as a catalyst for a multilayered regional system consisting of inter-Korean and other bilateral relations, the Four-Party Talks, a Six-Party forum, and an expanded ASEAN (Association of Southeast Asian Nations) Regional Forum. Within this system, each level has its own functions and roles.

Fourth, as long as both parties are committed to the principle of peaceful coexistence, "Korean-centeredness" in diplomacy toward the peninsula should be encouraged.

CHAPTER IX

Trilateral Relations and the Korean Peninsula

Scott Snyder

THE KOREAN PENINSULA has historically been a battleground, both in terms of influence and military conflict, among major powers in Asia, the vortex of political confrontation and competition for great power dominance from the end of the nineteenth century through the cold war. Each of the major powers involved on the Korean peninsula has a mixed historical legacy too fresh to be easily forgotten or fully overcome, and this unresolved legacy forms the basis for concern over the possible reemergence of a major power conflict in Northeast Asia today.

Ironically, under current circumstances each of the Korean peninsula's Pacific Rim neighbors finds to varying degrees that their respective short-term interests coincide in favor of maintaining a division between North and South Korea (or at least a gradual process of convergence between the two) and that the sudden reunification of Korea could, many fear, reignite tensions among the major powers in Northeast Asia. Indeed, positive China-U.S. relations—and, to a lesser degree, cooperative Sino-Japanese relations—are widely believed to be prerequisites for progress between the two Koreas. However, the status quo between North and South Korea is increasingly unsustainable despite the major powers' interest in a stabilized Korean peninsula, leaving open the possibility that renewed conflicts could develop accidentally in response to any sudden Korean reunification.

Although the shared short-term emphasis on stability by the major powers provides a basis for regional cooperation on Korean issues, their long-term views of the role and significance of the Korean peninsula may not coincide. This may lead to potential competition for influence on the Korean peninsula between China and the United States and between China and Japan. China, Japan, and the United States (and, to a lesser extent, Russia) have begun to hedge their bets in consideration of long-term interests, leading to the emergence of both new forms of cooperation and precursors of competition affecting the Korean peninsula. In addition, the strategic alignments and interests of a reunified Korea itself will be critical factors in determining the balance of power in Northeast Asia in the twenty-first century.

TRILATERAL SHORT-TERM COOPERATION TOWARD THE KOREAN PENINSULA

The short-term interests of China, Japan, and the United States toward the Korean peninsula have crystallized in recent years around three "no's": no war, no nuclear weapons development on the Korean peninsula, and no collapse of North Korea (the Democratic People's Republic of Korea). Limited forms of cooperation have emerged in support of these three policy objectives following the end of the cold war. For instance, with the normalization of relations between China and South Korea (the Republic of Korea) in 1992, Beijing first developed a policy of equal distance between the two Koreas, with an increasing emphasis on maintaining stability as a fundamental objective. China's support for continuing the Military Armistice Commission at Panmunjom, despite North Korean attempts to undermine it, and China's constructive role in the Four-Party Talks, which were designed to bring a lasting peace to the Korean peninsula, are two examples of Beijing's emphasis on stability as a priority over equidistance. This focus has brought China, the United States, and South

Korea into greater tactical alignment in response to any possible North Korean act of aggression. Japan has also been playing a supporting role through the strengthening of the Guidelines for U.S.-Japan Defense Cooperation to provide enhanced Japanese logistical support for U.S. troops in South Korea in the event of an outbreak of hostilities.

The emergence of the North Korean nuclear threat as a focus of global attention in 1993 and 1994 required new forms of cooperation involving China, Japan, the United States, and South Korea to counter North Korean actions. The initial limits of regional cooperation were clearly demonstrated by the inability of the United States to garner support for a sanctions drive against North Korea at the United Nations in 1993. However, negotiations between the United States and North Korea (as endorsed by the UN Security Council) to resolve international concerns about the North Korean nuclear weapons program required unprecedented diplomatic coordination to support both the outcome of the negotiations and the implementation of a long-term solution, as embodied by the North Korea-U.S. Geneva Agreed Framework of 1994.

Most notably, the negotiation process led to the establishment of a periodic trilateral diplomatic dialogue among Japan, the United States, and South Korea. In addition, implementation of the terms of the Agreed Framework through construction of proliferation-resistant light-water reactors in North Korea resulted in the establishment of the Korean Peninsula Energy Development Organization (KEDO), an international organization led by Japan, the United States, South Korea, and the European Union. Although China has been unwilling to officially join KEDO, Beijing has clearly indicated its support for the aims of KEDO and has demonstrated directly to Pyongyang its concerns regarding North Korea's nuclear weapons program. Indeed, China's support has widely been regarded as a critical prerequisite for the successful conclusion of North Korea-U.S. negotiations in Geneva. (Close cooperation within KEDO has also resulted in certain strains, most notably recent conflicts over funding of the project among Japan, the United States, and South Korea.)

As another example of cooperation, the international community has provided food aid to North Korea, in part to forestall potential refugee flows. However, regional coordination mechanisms in response to a possible collapse of the North Korean state remain limited. The international community, led by the United States, has responded to North Korea's humanitarian crisis through the UN World Food Program (WFP) by providing food aid, both out of a desire to lessen the risk of political instability in North Korea and for humanitarian reasons. China has acted independently of the international community, but it has been North Korea's largest food donor, primarily for security reasons—to prevent refugees from spilling over into Chinese provinces bordering North Korea. The United States has been one of the largest donors to the WFP, which launched its largest appeal ever in 1997, raising US$415 million to allay North Korea's food crisis. Japan, for domestic political reasons, has not made a significant contribution, despite holding large stockpiles of aging grain. Contingency planning for the possibility of a North Korean collapse has been initiated by Japan, the United States, and South Korea.

Policy coordination activities by China, Japan, and the United States in response to overlapping short-term interests in favor of maintaining stability on the Korean peninsula suggest that such efforts are partial and ad hoc rather than comprehensive and institutionalized. There is still no official subregional dialogue mechanism devoted primarily to security in Northeast Asia; KEDO offers the best example of concrete cooperation in pursuit of a clearly defined, practical objective. Notable discrepancies in short-term responses to North Korea's challenge include China's unwillingness to formally join KEDO, the major instrument for cooperation to attain nonproliferation objectives on the Korean peninsula, and Japan's unwillingness to contribute food aid to North Korea as part of the international humanitarian aid effort because of its own domestic political constraints. (Negative public opinion in Japan over alleged North Korean kidnappings of Japanese nationals in the 1960s and 1970s has made it more difficult to reach consensus in Japan on any policy initiative toward North Korea.) For the United States, the major policy challenge is to maintain effective policy coordination among Japan, South Korea, and the United States to pursue joint policies despite a differing order of priorities while also continuing to reach out to China for additional support in coaxing North Korea toward greater engagement with the outside world.

Long-Term Views on the Korean Peninsula

Despite the development of limited cooperation among China, Japan, and the United States on Korea-related issues resulting from shared short-term interests in stability, differing long-term strategic interests toward the Korea peninsula may lead to future competition as each of the three countries seeks to extend its influence on the Korean peninsula. China and Japan have overlapping but conflicting security interests on the Korean peninsula because of uncertainty as to whether the Koreas are a security buffer or a security threat, depending on the quality of their respective bilateral relations with Korean leaders. The U.S. interest on the Korean peninsula stems from global interests in the maintenance of security and stability in a conflict-prone region and from a healthy economic relationship with South Korea. However, a continuing U.S. presence in post-reunification Korea may be perceived negatively by a rising China with its own version of a Monroe Doctrine for former tributary states and near neighbors. Thus, the future orientation of Korea as a neutral party or as a nation that tilts toward China, Japan, or the United States will be perceived as a key factor in determining the long-term security environment in the region. As it has become clear that Seoul is more likely than Pyongyang to shape the future orientation of a reunified Korea, the emphasis placed by neighboring governments, including Beijing, on establishing strong relationships with the Korean leadership in Seoul has shifted accordingly.

The challenge for the United States is how to retain influence on the Korean peninsula while managing a peaceful transition to a unified and democratic Korea. Such a policy requires an emphasis on maintaining strong South Korea-U.S. relations and on supporting South Korean efforts to reduce inter-Korean tensions. To the extent that Seoul is willing to engage in an accommodating policy that supports North Korea's integration with the outside world, the United States should support such an effort, developing relations with Pyongyang in tandem with improvements in inter-Korean relations. The

U.S. role in helping to reduce tensions on the Korean peninsula is indispensable, particularly given the fact that, although limited, the United States may have more potential influence in Pyongyang than any other government. Nevertheless, U.S. influence in Pyongyang is most effective when implemented with Seoul in the lead.

The United States must lead the international community in support of Seoul's attempts to conduct a generous, inclusive policy toward North Korea, without being seen as either obstructionist or irrelevant. In other words, the key to sustaining U.S. objectives and influence on the Korean peninsula is to maintain strong security relations with Seoul, without taking an overbearing approach, up to and even after Korean reunification. Such an approach requires careful management of sensitive Japan-Korea relations. The United States should avoid any action that suggests to Koreans that Tokyo is a more important partner than Seoul and should encourage the harmonization of objectives and functions of the Japan-U.S. and South Korea-U.S. security alliances as basic to regional stability.

China's efforts to support near-term stability on the Korean peninsula are entirely consistent with its long-term objectives of maintaining a security buffer on its border and increasing China's economic and political influence in both Koreas. Although some Chinese scholars now predict that North Korea's collapse is inevitable, a policy that seeks to delay North Korea's disintegration and subsequent Korean reunification through provision of food aid while expanding China's economic and political influence in Pyongyang and Seoul serves China's near-term security interests. This includes nurturing trade and economic relations with Seoul, although the rapid growth of this relationship has suffered in the fallout from the Asian financial crisis.

China's sensitivity to the dominant U.S. role on the Korean peninsula is a factor inhibiting long-term China-U.S. cooperation on Korean issues. Any outcome on the Korean peninsula that appears to expand U.S. influence in the region will not be welcome in Beijing. However, although Chinese policymakers may prefer that U.S. troops leave the Korean peninsula after reunification, China's ability to influence such an event under current circumstances remains circumscribed; it is not in a position to veto the perpetuation of a long-standing security relationship with the United States if the leadership of a reunified Korea so chooses. In the end, the only viable

Chinese strategy for reducing U.S. influence on the Korean peninsula is to gain as much economic and political influence as possible in Seoul in an attempt to convince Seoul to choose Beijing over Washington.

Japan's long-term political influence on the Korean peninsula appears to be the weakest and most indirect among Korea's Pacific Rim neighbors, although Japan will remain an indispensable economic partner for Korea's reconstruction, and improvements in South Korea-Japan military cooperation demonstrate pragmatic and guarded willingness to cooperate despite past differences. A major security concern will be the maintenance of a good relationship between Japan and Korea. Recent disputes over maritime sovereignty and fishing rights are indications that Japanese-Korean relations may become more troubled as the inter-Korean confrontation subsides or following Korea's reunification. Such friction could diminish Japan's political influence on the Korean peninsula, although strong economic ties may help to dampen political tensions. The strengthening of U.S. security relationships with Tokyo and Seoul is another factor that could temper such tensions by reinforcing the recent trend toward military exchange and cooperation between Japan and South Korea. The difficulty for Japan's leaders will be how to gain political credit for its economic contributions toward Korea's reconstruction without being perceived as competing with China for economic or political influence.

Given these opportunities for both cooperation and confrontation, the choices made on the Korean peninsula will play an important role in defining the future nature of security relations in Northeast Asia among China, Japan, and the United States. Ironically, the prospects for trilateral cooperation on Korean issues are greater whereas the prospects for a reunified Korea remain dim, but as the likelihood of Korean reunification grows, competition among Korea's neighbors for influence over the process will likely increase. As occurred at the end of the nineteenth century, a unified Korea may again be the vortex for great power competition in Northeast Asia. But this time, the choices made by the Korean government—even if it is preoccupied with problems of internal reconstruction and reintegration—may also influence the future direction of international relations in the region. Although there is no guarantee that the Korean-U.S. security relationship will be extended, the most likely Korean choice will be to seek assistance from its least threatening, most distant ally—a partner able to provide balance in a complex regional environment and defend against the potential threat of near neighbors. However, Korean public attitudes, Congressional views of the U.S. troop presence in Asia, China's posture, and the level of tensions in Japan-Korea relations will all have a bearing on Korea's tactical choices, as Korea engages in a familiar historical gambit of playing off big powers against each other to perpetuate its survival and influence on its own terms.

About the Contributors

EVAN A. FEIGENBAUM is a Fellow at the Robert and Renee Belfer Center for Science and International Affairs, John F. Kennedy School of Government, Harvard University. He has also taught Chinese foreign policy and the history of the nuclear age at Harvard as a Lecturer on Government in the Faculty of Arts and Sciences, and served as Program Chair of the Kennedy School's Executive Program for Senior Chinese Military Officers. Dr. Feigenbaum received his Ph.D. in political science from Stanford University in 1997. From 1994 to 1997, he was a fellow at Stanford's Center for International Security and Arms Control, and he was a John M. Olin Postdoctoral Fellow in National Security at Harvard in 1997–1998. In 1994–1995, he taught on the faculty of the U.S. Naval Postgraduate School. He writes on Chinese defense and technology policy, U.S.-China relations, and the management of innovation in high-technology industries, including issues of corporate governance and public versus private-equity strategies of technology finance. His recent publications include articles in *International Security*, *Survival*, and the *China Quarterly*, as well as the book *Change in Taiwan and Potential Adversity in the Strait* (1995). He is now preparing a forthcoming book on the impact of strategic weapons and other large-scale national high-technology programs on China's political and economic development. He is currently a Term Member of the Council on Foreign Relations.

NI FENG is Associate Research Fellow of the Institute of American Studies, Chinese Academy of Social Sciences (CASS). He earned his B.A. from the Department of International Politics, Peking University.

He is currently a Ph.D. candidate at the graduate school with CASS. He has been engaged in advanced studies on Japan-U.S. relations with the Japan Institute of International Affairs, where he was a visiting fellow in 1995. His research focuses on American political thinking and Sino-American relations. As part of his research work, he participated in the national project "China, the United States, and Japan Triangle Relations" and the CASS priority program "The Clinton Administration's Foreign Policy." At present, he is involved in research on U.S.-Japan security relations after the redefinition of the U.S.-Japan Security Treaty. Mr. Ni has published more than one hundred articles on international affairs in newspapers, magazines, and journals since 1988.

FUNABASHI YŌICHI is Chief Diplomatic Correspondent and Columnist and former Washington Bureau Chief for the *Asahi Shimbun*. He has covered politics and economics in Japan and has been the *Asahi* correspondent in Washington, D.C., and Beijing, and a Nieman Fellow at Harvard University. Dr. Funabashi was an Ushiba Fellow in 1986 and was a fellow at the Institute for International Economics in 1987. He is the author of numerous books, including *Japan's International Agenda* (1994), *An Emerging China in a World of Independence* (co-author, 1994), and *Asia Pacific Fusion: Japan's Role in APEC* (1995). Winner of the Suntory Humanities Award of 1983 for *Neibu Inside China*, he was also awarded the 1985 Vaughn-Ueda Prize, often called Japan's Pulitzer Prize, for his coverage of U.S.-Japan economic friction, the Yoshino Sakuzō Prize in 1988 for his book *Managing the Dollar: From the Plaza to the Louvre*, and the Ishibashi Tanzan Prize in 1992 for his articles "Japan and the New World Order" for *Foreign Affairs* and "Japan and America: Global Partnership" for *Foreign Policy*. His most recent article, "Japan's Depression Diplomacy," appeared in *Foreign Affairs* in November 1998.

LEE JONG WON has been Professor of international politics at Rikkyo University since 1996. Currently, he is a visiting fellow at Princeton University. Prior to his current post, Dr. Lee was associate professor of international politics at Tohoku University. He earned his B.A. in political science from International Christian University in 1984, and his M.A. and Ph.D. in international politics from Tokyo

University in 1996. Before moving to Japan, Dr. Lee was a staff member of the Korean Student Christian Federation (1976–1978) and a researcher with the Christian Institute for the Study of Justice and Development (1978–1981). His major publications include "Cold War and Regionalism in East Asia" (1993) and *U.S.-Korean Relations and Japan in East Asia's Cold War* (1996), which was awarded the 1999 Foreign Language Book Prize by the Organization of American Historians.

DANIEL H. ROSEN is Research Fellow at the Institute for International Economies in Washington, D.C. He has focused on the economic development of East Asia, particularly emerging Greater China. He is now studying the commercial concerns of foreign-invested enterprises in mainland China, and the policy responses needed to address those concerns. Other areas of focus include telecommunications negotiations, trade and environment linkages, and the limits of economic sanctions as a foreign policy tool.

SCOTT SNYDER is an Asia specialist in the Research and Studies Program of the United States Institute of Peace. Mr. Snyder recently completed a study as part of the Institute's project on cross-cultural negotiation tentatively entitled *Negotiating on the Edge: Patterns in North Korea's Diplomatic Style*. He received his B.A. from Rice University in 1987 and his M.A. from the Regional Studies East Asia Program at Harvard University in 1990. He was an Abe Fellow at the Japan Institute of International Affairs and the Asia Forum Japan in 1998–1999. As part of his Abe Fellowship research project on aspects of policy coordination among the United States, Japan, and South Korea and the implications for security in Northeast Asia, he spent time in Tokyo, Seoul, and Beijing during that year. He has written extensively on Korean affairs and has also conducted research on the political/security implications of the Asian financial crisis and on regional island disputes in Asia, including the conflicting maritime claims in the South China Sea.

WATANABE KŌJI is Executive Advisor to the Japan Federation of Economic Organizations (Keidanren) and Senior Fellow at the Japan Center for International Exchange. He was Japanese ambassador to Russia from 1993 to 1996 and ambassador to Italy from 1992 to 1993. He was also deputy minister for foreign affairs, sherpa for the G-7 Houston and London summits of 1990 and 1991, and Japanese cochairman of the U.S.-Japan Structural Impediments Initiative Talks. Ambassador Watanabe joined the Foreign Ministry upon graduating from the University of Tokyo in 1956 and served as director-general of the Information Analysis, Research and Planning Bureau and director-general of the Economic Affairs Bureau. He was a visiting fellow at the Woodrow Wilson School of Princeton University (1957–1958) and at the Center for International Affairs of Harvard University (1973–1974). His other overseas posts include counsellor at the Japanese Embassy in Saigon (1974–1976), minister at the Japanese Embassy in Beijing (1981–1984), and ambassador to Saudi Arabia (1988–1989).

YANG JIEMIAN is Director and Senior Fellow of the Department of American Studies, Shangai Institute for International Studies (SIIS). He is Council Director of the China Association of American Studies, China Association of Sino-U.S. Relations and the Shanghai Association of International Strategic Studies, and Standing Director of the Shanghai Association of International Relations. He has published many books and papers on international relations and American foreign policy. His most recent publications include *Sino-U.S. Relations in the Post–Cold War Era: Elaboration and Exploration* (1997); "Sino-U.S. Relations towards the 21st Century: Changes and Challenges," in the *SIIS Journal* (April 1997); and "Summit Diplomacy and Strategic Partnership: Aspirations, Expectations, and Realization," in *The Outlook for U.S.-China Relations Following the 1997–1998 Summits: Chinese and American Perspectives on Security, Trade, and Cultural Exchange* (1999). Mr. Yang received his B.A. from the Shanghai Teacher's University in 1979, his M.A. in international relations from SIIS in 1981, and his M.A. in international relations from the Fletcher School of Law and Diplomacy in 1984.

Index

Japan Center for International Exchange

FOUNDED IN 1970, the Japan Center for International Exchange (JCIE) is an independent, nonprofit, and nonpartisan organization dedicated to strengthening Japan's role in international affairs. JCIE believes that Japan faces a major challenge in augmenting its positive contributions to the international community, in keeping with its position as one of the world's largest industrial democracies. Operating in a country where policy making has traditionally been dominated by the government bureaucracy, JCIE has played an important role in broadening debate on Japan's international responsibilities by conducting international and cross-sectional programs of exchange, research, and discussion.

JCIE creates opportunities for informed policy discussions; it does not take policy positions. JCIE programs are carried out with the collaboration and cosponsorship of many organizations. The contacts developed through these working relationships are crucial to JCIE's efforts to increase the number of Japanese from the private sector engaged in meaningful policy research and dialogue with overseas counterparts. JCIE receives no government subsidies; rather, funding comes from private foundation grants, corporate contributions, and contracts.